'It is always refreshing to read a book that brings ... .
table, alongside valuing all that has gone before . . . Anne Richards
explores some fresh lines of thinking and understanding of the
Scriptures in relation to children. Her five themes of calling, life and
salvation, commissioning, healing and blessing take us into fresh
ways of ensuring that children are seen as fully human and fully part
of the people of God, even from the womb. *Children in the Bible* is not
just for those concerned about children in society and the Church – it
is for all leaders who want to take being human seriously.'

The Rt Revd Paul Butler, Bishop of Southwell and Nottingham,
and Children's Advocate for the Church of England

'This is a hugely important book. It is all too easy to assume that
the Bible's treatment of children is either monochrome or overly
sentimental. Here Anne Richards presents us with an altogether
richer, deeper and broader picture in which children stand right at
the heart of God's vision for the world.'

Dr Paula Gooder, writer and lecturer in biblical studies

'An outstanding and undoubtedly "fresh approach" to what childhood suggests about God and what God suggests about childhood.
Arising from thorough and original theological reflection on the
surprisingly many ways in which childhood and children appear
in the Scriptures, Anne Richards provides so much more than a
book merely about "children in the Bible". She calls us to discern
the profundity of God's purposes embedded in the universal human
experience of being a child, and to consider what a theology of
childhood means for relating to children today.'

Dr Rebecca Nye, lecturer and researcher in children's
spirituality, and lead UK consultant of Godly Play

For Chris Corrigan,
and for JJ and Pip

CHILDREN IN THE BIBLE

A fresh approach

ANNE RICHARDS

First published in Great Britain in 2013

Society for Promoting Christian Knowledge
36 Causton Street
London SW1P 4ST
www.spckpublishing.co.uk

British Library Cataloguing-in-Publication Data
A catalogue record for this book is available from the British Library

ISBN 978–0–281–06688–9
eBook ISBN 978–0–281–06689–6

Typeset by Graphicraft Limited, Hong Kong
First printed in Great Britain by Ashford Colour Press
Subsequently digitally printed in Great Britain

Produced on paper from sustainable forests

Contents

About the author

Dr Anne Richards is National Adviser for mission theology, alternative spiritualities and new religious movements for the Archbishops' Council of the Church of England. She is the convener of the Mission Theology Advisory Group, which provides churches with resources for spirituality, theology, reconciliation, evangelism and mission. Previously, she combined an academic life teaching literature in Oxford with working in a hospital, and she has long experience of working with and writing about children and young people. She is also a trustee of Godly Play UK and (with Peter Privett) co-edited *Through the Eyes of a Child* (Church House Publishing, 2009).

Acknowledgements

I am grateful to the Archbishops' Council of the Church of England for a period of long service leave in 2012, which enabled me to pay concentrated attention to drafting this book. I have also been greatly helped in the production of this book by Tracey Messenger at SPCK and by Audrey Mann.

All the arguments and opinions expressed in this book are my own and I am solely responsible for any mistakes or omissions. However, many people have helped me form the ideas for this book and I want to acknowledge their friendship, guidance and wise advice.

I am thankful for the friendship and help of colleagues at the National Church Institutions and especially to successive National Advisers for children's work. I have also had many fruitful conversations with diocesan children's advisers. Thanks are also due to the trustees of Godly Play UK and those of their network who have given me insights into working with children, and to all my friends and colleagues in the Mission Theology Advisory Group.

Not least I want to pay tribute to all the children and young people I've worked with over the years who have both challenged and inspired me in equal measure. But there are a few children whose stories especially find their way into these pages. So thanks and love are due especially to Jonathan and Philip, Eden, Jude, and Matthew and George.

Introduction

A child asks God a hard question

In 2011, the journalist Alex Renton wrote an article about how his six-year-old daughter wanted to ask God 'who invented you?'[1] Renton himself did not feel able to help with the question, or indeed, how to go about asking God, so he sent the enquiry to various churches, including the Church of England at Lambeth Palace in London. A little while later, Lulu received a letter from Dr Rowan Williams, who was then Archbishop of Canterbury. It read:

Dear Lulu,
Your dad has sent on your letter and asked if I have any answers. It's a difficult one! But I think God might reply a bit like this –

'Dear Lulu – Nobody invented me – but lots of people discovered me and were quite surprised. They discovered me when they looked round at the world and thought it was really beautiful or really mysterious and wondered where it came from. They discovered me when they were very very quiet on their own and felt a sort of peace and love they hadn't expected.

Then they invented ideas about me – some of them sensible and some of them not very sensible. From time to time I sent them some hints – specially in the life of Jesus – to help them get closer to what I'm really like.

But there was nothing and nobody around before me to invent me. Rather like somebody who writes a story in a book, I started making up the story of the world and eventually invented human beings like you who could ask me awkward questions!'

And then he'd send you lots of love and sign off.

I know he doesn't usually write letters, so I have to do the best I can on his behalf. Lots of love from me too.

+Archbishop Rowan

In its simplicity, generosity and directness, this letter embodies many of the things I think are important for a book about God's relationship

---

[1] A. Renton, 'A Letter to God – and a Reply from Lambeth', *The Times*, 22 April 2011.

to children. First, the Archbishop suggests that finding out and asking questions about God is important and all such questions deserve to be taken seriously, whether we are children or adults. Such questions may certainly be difficult and awkward and lead us to confusing and baffling places, but that is not an excuse to avoid them or to give up on the search to find out what we can know and what we can say (which might not be the same thing). Neither should we shy away from the sheer difficulty of making sense of God. Second, the journey of spirituality includes discovery, surprise, beauty, mystery, and personal experiences of peace and love. Recognizing that these things are both experienced and recognized by children and have spiritual value is also important. God is not 'out there' at some immeasurable distance, but discoverable within our world and within ourselves. Rowan Williams presents God as the eternal storyteller, whose rich, unfolding narrative brings people into being who can recognize and ask big questions of the Creator. But there is a warning too – that people have also 'invented ideas' about God which are 'not very sensible'. This means that part of the discovery of God is to find *trustworthy* means of finding out what God is like and what God's purpose is for human beings. Rowan Williams notes that for Christians, the person and ministry of Jesus especially offer that route to knowing God.

What I most like about the letter, though, is that while the focus is a young child, Rowan Williams becomes an amanuensis, allowing *God* to speak, doing 'the best he can' to put the child in touch with her divine correspondent. This is at the heart of theology, not to prescribe (or proscribe) on behalf of God, or to create God in our own image, or to use God as an excuse for making people do as we want them to do, but simply to create a space where something of God can be understood.

In this book, I will try to do the same. There are many wonderful books written about children, about children and the Church, and about children in the context of faith. But it seems to me that there is often something missing; we very easily make assumptions about what God is about in all this, or if it's too complicated, simply leave God out of the mix altogether.

I want to ask what we can know and what we can say (if anything) about God's relation to children, and then to ask what difference that theological enquiry might make to the complex issues which face us as children, parents and communities in today's world. I want to do that by reframing issues from the starting point of the child. The results might be surprising. They might also be challenging. They might lead us to places where there are no answers to our questions and we will have to look through the options for the best possible way to grapple with what confronts and baffles us.

The question then arises: where can we find more letters from God? For Christians, our personal sense-making ability and our experience as human beings bring vital evidence to bear. The long tradition of Christian history and Christian community also gives us material to reflect on and evaluate together. But at the heart of the Christian tradition, Scripture offers God's story. Scripture is of course made up of extraordinary texts including, among other things, history, poetry, dramatic allegory, lament, chronicle, law, testimony, letters and sheer overwhelming mystery, with a host of different writers doing the best they can to offer windows into God's world so that we can see God at work. And in God's world, we find that children have a very particular and special place, not just as part of God's story but also as *makers* of God's story, the providers to us of a language through which God's will for the creation is revealed.

To do that, I have offered five words, one for each of the following chapters, which I suggest represent the God-language manifested to us by and through children. At the heart of this I will show that children are worth God's special attention and that they are deeply woven into God's purposes. I want to see how far we can find evidence that, according to Scripture, overlooked and under-represented children, both in the Bible and in our contemporary world, are found worthy by God. They are found worthy of calling, salvation, commission, healing and blessing. That search will also have to take place in the knowledge of a background reality in the world of the Bible of many, many children whose lives are blighted, damaged or destroyed. For them, too, there must be some account, as the God-language they mediate into the world is twisted, ruined or obliterated.

I also want to look at how the idea of being a child or children of the Father becomes embedded into the self-description of the early church, a church of brothers and sisters, of a young family looking forward to growing up in God's reconciled world.

Struggling with Scripture

How are we supposed to read Scripture? Robert Alter, Professor of Hebrew and Comparative Literature in the Department of Near Eastern Studies, University of California, Berkeley, tells us that interpretation of the Bible is a never-ending process because the texts are so rich and diverse. However, he does caution that when anyone offers commentary or discussion of the Bible it should be done in a way that 'instead of submerging the text under the weight of erudition actually helps us to read the text more fully'.[2] How can we do this? In Genesis, the first book of the Bible, there is a dramatic, profound and mysterious story (32.23–33). It concerns the famous Hebrew patriarch Jacob. We know from the buildup to this story that Jacob is the younger twin brother of Esau,[3] and that he has stolen from his brother both his birthright and blessing. Now Jacob is about to meet his brother again and he is terrified of his brother's vengeful anger and possible retribution. In the pitch black of night, alone and afraid, on what might be his last night on earth, Jacob has a fight with a mysterious 'man'. They struggle and wrestle together. The fight in the darkness isn't just a dream; Jacob is physically injured and ends up limping. Because the 'man' does not overcome Jacob, Jacob holds on to him and refuses to let go until the stranger gives him a blessing. The stranger tells him that he is going to give Jacob another name – Israel, meaning the one who has struggled with God and prevailed. Jacob also names the place where this struggle has taken place: Peniel, meaning 'I have seen God face to face, and yet my life is preserved'.

This event has profound and lasting effects. Jacob believes that by applying himself in the struggle he has met God face to face and lived, something which is supposed to be impossible, and this supernatural encounter has utterly changed him. Jacob becomes a new person, whose future is invested in a holy community; he is

---

[2] R. Alter, 'Scripture, Commentary and the Challenge of Interpretation', in A. Weiner and L. Kaplan (eds), *Graven Images – on Interpretation: Studies In Culture, Law, and the Sacred* (Madison, WI: University of Wisconsin Press, 2002), p. 27.

[3] We will see that scriptural narratives often have two children or paired children, or paired stories which reflect one another.

spiritually changed and he also goes out to an extraordinary and powerful reconciliation with his brother.

I think that this story tells us a great deal about what it should be like to read Scripture. Reading Scripture is, or should be, a struggle, a wrestling, with a rich, maddening and complex text, whose patterns, meanings and textures are often so difficult to discern. When we really engage with Scripture we can be like Jacob, alone in the dark, battling with strangeness, trying not to be overwhelmed. That's true even if we are very familiar with the Bible, at home with its well-known stories and language. Sometimes we forget that it is always much deeper, richer and more troubling than we allow.

Yet the struggle leads to something really important. We cannot say for certain who it is Jacob struggles with – is it himself, his conscience, a man, an angel, God? The struggle can lead to all these conclusions, but the exact answer does not really matter. We can see that it is in the act of encounter that Jacob comes to understand something about himself and something about God. First Jacob has to be literally put out of joint, dislocated from his presuppositions. His own life is given new purpose and meaning, but this is not just a private revelation, it changes the way his future life with his family and his people works.

So reading Scripture and wrestling for its meaning offers these possibilities. The history we bring to the encounter is different for each one of us and can be conditioned by scepticism, a feeling of inadequacy, by love, or by faith, or even by all of these. Yet the encounter holds out the possibility that at the end of the struggle with words and meanings we will know more about the story and purpose of God, and that learning will make us think more profoundly about what that story means for the world in which we live. We are asked to find ways of 'unfolding its meanings, illuminating its dark places, sorting out its seeming ambiguities, explaining its implications'.[4]

For some Christians, the New Testament is the most important part of the Bible to read and less weight may be given to Old Testament literature. I know some Christians who can quote vast amounts of the New Testament by heart but who never spend any time on the rest of the Bible. But I believe that it is very important to struggle

---

[4] Alter, 'Scripture, Commentary and the Challenge of Interpretation', p. 22.

with the Hebrew Scriptures as well. These were, after all, Jesus' own biblical texts and he steeped himself in them, reading them, teaching out of them, interpreting them for the people around him. So did the Apostles and Paul. If we want to know what Jesus is doing in his words and actions in the Gospels, then seeking to understand his own engagement with Scripture is for me also an act of discipleship.

There are some other issues of which we need to be aware. As the Bible was not written in English it can be difficult to know exactly what words translated as 'infant', 'child', 'children', 'youth', and so on really mean and in places I have suggested that the words offered in well-known translations might be misleading. Also, while there are different names for God in Scripture, and those differences are important for exegetical purposes, I prefer simply to call God 'God', wherever possible without gender attributions. In quoting from the New Testament, I have typically used the New Revised Standard Version. In referring to extracts from the Hebrew Scriptures (Old Testament), I have wherever possible used translations by the same Robert Alter, noted above, which have been particularly helpful to me in understanding better the role of God in the history of the world.

The shape of this book

There are five chapters in this book, each of which concentrates on an aspect of what God wants for the lives of children. Each chapter also focuses on a word (be, grow, act, whole, grace) in which I find God-language manifested to us by and through children. At the end of each chapter are a number of questions, which may be used by individuals or by groups studying the book together. There is also a suggested 'Activity', which can be used to make a small but positive change in your own life, your church or community. I conclude the book with some final reflections.

At the end of the book is an Appendix listing words associated with the idea of 'child' in the Bible, and a list of significant Scripture passages which refer to children.

1

God finds children worthy of calling

'Be . . .'

I once had a conversation with a nun in which she told me that she had
been convinced of her calling on the day she took her First Holy Communion at the age of seven. I was sceptical, because I could imagine that
all the teaching and preparation for the event, the making of a special
dress, the drama of the occasion, all the fuss and attention, the mystery
and sacredness, that sheer sacramental power of the first Eucharist,
could very well make a powerful impression on a young child. But was
this powerful impression really God's will? Was there really a call?

'How did you know?' I asked. 'What happened?'

'God asked me,' she said, 'and I said yes.'

If anything this made me more intrigued. God spoke? How? And
how did a little child know this was God speaking? What did God
say? Weren't you scared? Did you tell anyone? Did you have this
experience once or many times?

'That's not the point,' she said, laughing. 'The point is: I am here.'

Gently, she was telling me that I was looking to pinpoint and
analyse something that was really a process, the choosing of a path
on a journey that matches a growing sense of purpose and rightness.
But more to the point, she was telling me that her journey was
shaped by an experience in childhood; it was as a child that God
found her worthy of call and powerful, loving response.

The hymn that is often sung at First Holy Communion services has
the words 'Here I am, Lord. Is it I, Lord? I have heard you calling in the
night', based on the call of the child Samuel in 1 Samuel 3. In these words
and in the nun's story, we learn some important things about how
God finds children worthy of calling, and when we turn to Scripture
we can find out a great deal more about how that calling happens.
First, that call is not necessarily something that comes from 'out there'
as many people instinctively imagine. Rather God's call to us can be

encountered deep within ourselves, a recognition that it is there in the depths of our being; it is intimate, ongoing, personal, loving, and ultimately transforming. It is also related to the fact of our being as embodied creatures and to the way we grow. Second, God's call only becomes something that focuses the direction of a person's life if at some point there is a response, a 'yes! I am here!' to the recognition that God is asking something of us, opening a pathway for us, creating and shaping a place for us to be in the power of the Spirit. Third, being part of a fellowship of believers helps to make space for that vocation to be recognized, encouraged and acknowledged. How vocation happens, whether as a 'voice', a dream, a gradual conviction, discernment of God's presence, or recognition by others that God is shaping a person's life, is unimportant. What matters is that all are called, and that there is a point when a person comes to a decision to be obedient to that calling, in the words of Isaiah: 'Here am I; send me!' (Isaiah 6.8).

In this chapter I want to reframe the idea of 'call' and suggest that Scripture gives us insight into how God calls us into being from our earliest beginnings. I will suggest that human growth and development is of itself a response to God's call. I also want to look at how, when children become aware of God's active presence in their lives, this leads to a presenting of the self before God which is both a 'yes!' and 'I am here'.

God calls us into being

If we look into Scripture to find out more about how God finds children worthy of call, we immediately encounter an extraordinary prospect: that if God calls us to be, then God also calls us into being and these two divine purposes are mixed together. The 'yes!' in response to God's work in a person's life is preceded by a biological 'yes!' as the new person comes into being. This is perhaps echoed in the assertion in Galatians 1.15: 'God . . . set me [Paul] apart before I was born and called me through his grace'. It is not surprising, then, that in both Jeremiah and Isaiah, the prophetic vocation is traced back to a time before birth.

> Now the word of the LORD came to me, saying,
> 'Before I formed you in the womb I knew you,
> And before you were born I

Consecrated you;
Appointed you a prophet to the nations.'

(Jeremiah 1.4–5)

The LORD called me before I was born,
While I was in my mother's womb he named me.
He made my mouth like a sharp sword,
In the shadow of his hand he hid me;
He made me a polished arrow,
In his quiver he hid me away.
And he said to me, 'You are my servant,
Israel, in whom I will be glorified.'

(Isaiah 49.1b–3)

The writer of this passage of Jeremiah imagines that God's relationship with the prophet began before his birth. He was known, loved and made special. The writer of this part of Isaiah offers us beautiful images for the love relationship between God and the unborn child: he is an arrow who has been lovingly polished and crafted, protected by the shadow of God's hand, given a name and a destiny and a purpose. Both these passages suggest that the prophetic vocation is part of a divine calling that begins to unfold from conception. There is another passage of Scripture which tells us more about God's relationship with the unborn child. The psalmist tells us:

For it was you who formed my inward parts;
You knit me together in my mother's womb.
I praise you, for I am fearfully and wonderfully made.
Wonderful are your works;
That I know very well.
My frame was not hidden from you,
When I was being made in secret,
Intricately woven in the depths of the earth [i.e. the womb].
Your eyes beheld my unformed substance.
In your book were written
All the days that were formed for me,
When none of them as yet existed.

(Psalm 139.13–16)

The language here is of making, forming, knitting together, but there is more to it than that. There is a sense of God being at the heart of the new individual's being, watching over it, being intimately involved in the child's becoming, loving him and calling him into birth and the life that God desires for him. This suggests that every newly conceived person has a rightness and goodness in God's eyes which echoes the goodness God sees in the whole creation (Genesis 1.31). What happens to the child when she is born, whether into poverty, a vastly overpopulated world, with disabilities, or subject to illness and suffering, is another matter which will be looked at in other chapters of this book. The essential point is that God loves and is involved with every new human being that is conceived and has a loving purpose for them, irrespective of what actually happens to them in an imperfect world. What then can we say about the mysterious beginnings of each of us?

How we begin

Embryogenesis is an extraordinary sequence of events which most people know very little about. Although all of us have gone through the process in the womb which makes us what we are, and all mothers who have given birth have directly experienced pregnancy, we tend to know very little about what our earliest moments were like, or what was happening to the developing child in the womb. Books on pregnancy may give information about what the developing foetus looks like at different weeks into the pregnancy, and pregnant women and their partners in many societies are usually offered scans which allow them to see their unborn children, but they may have little idea how their developing children came to be like that. Yet embryo-genesis is marvellous, mysterious and extraordinarily beautiful. To give a sense of this I will draw on Armand Marie Leroi's account of embryological beginnings in his book *Mutants*, because he combines a scientific account with striking images which convey to us the beauty and mystery of what occurs in early life.[1]

When sperm meets egg, the resulting conceptus begins immediately to divide until it forms a ball of about 100 cells. Leroi then tells us: 'On the seventh day after conception, a human embryo begins to dig . . .

---

[1] A. Leroi, *Mutants: On the Form, Varieties and Errors of the Human Body* (London: HarperCollins, 2003).

Most of the cells in the hollow ball are occupied with the business of burrowing, but some are up to other things. They are beginning to organise themselves into a ball of their own so that by day 9 the embryo is rather like one of those ingenious Chinese toys composed of carved ivory spheres within spheres within spheres.'[2]

What this communicates to us is a sense of purposeful becoming at the deepest cellular level: complexity is emerging and organization is already taking place. At the point where the 'primitive streak' appears, about 13 days after conception, Leroi describes how 'Cells migrate towards the streak and pour themselves into it' giving a sense of energy and urgency in the earliest becoming of the new individual.[3] The embryo becomes organized into three layers, all of which are destined for future roles in our bodies. The top layer will be skin and the nervous system, the middle layer will become our muscles and bones, the bottom layer our organs, although other parts of the body will form from cells from different layers combined. Leroi then asks us to consider another miracle: that the embryo has both orientation and geometry: 'Two weeks after egg met sperm, the embryo has a head and a tail, a front and a back, a left and a right. The question is, how did it get them?'[4]

Leroi tells us that science has been able to show that embryonic development is dependent on signalling molecules which communicate across the body of the embryo, switching genes on and off and conveying instructions on what cells should become. But the strength of the signal also matters: 'the cells from our bodies must be continually bathed in many signals emanating from many sources. Some of these signals speak with one voice, but others offer conflicting advice.' The conflict is solved, according to the relative strength of the chemical signals: 'the fate of a given cell depends on the balance of the concentration between the two competing molecules'.[5] Leroi then goes on to make the following observation: 'In a way, the embryo is just a microcosm of the cognitive world we inhabit, the world of signals that insistently urge us to travel to one destination rather than another, eschew some goals in favour of others, hold some things to

---

[2] Leroi, *Mutants*, p. 36.
[3] Leroi, *Mutants*, p. 36.
[4] Leroi, *Mutants*, p. 37.
[5] Leroi, *Mutants*, p. 42.

be true and others false; in short that moulds us into what we are'. This is an interesting insight in that it prompts us to think of our existence before and after birth as a continuum in which the whole person is shaped and moulded by the process of becoming. Birth is just one event in that process. This can fit into a theological and biblical sense that God's presence is also intertwined with that process.

The result of this activity is a remarkable transformation. Leroi tells us that by day 19 the embryo resembles the 'elongate leaf of a tulip' which on day 21 has rolled up 'as a moth folds its wings' until it 'zips up' into a hollow tube becoming the rudiments of spinal column and brain. Organs and deep layers of skin begin to form around it and the abdominal tube also begins to form, one part of which 'will begin to twist and twist again to become a small machine of exquisite design . . . On day 21 it begins to beat.'[6]

I have suggested that Scripture tells us that God calls the child into being and therefore that this remarkable biological process is intimately entwined with that call. But we have to remember that we cannot assert that God directly assembles the developing foetus or 'designs' the individual child. The way that the events unfold, from the embedding of the 'digging' embryo into the lining of the womb, to the organization of its cells, the delicate response to chemical signals as the building blocks of organs and muscles and skin form, are a response to God's desire for a new individual to be. However, as Leroi's book on mutants makes abundantly clear, there are all kinds of things which can go wrong in such a delicate process; the biology is subject to many pitfalls and the resulting individual may not emerge with a perfect body. Essentially, too, we are all mutants. Yet God calls every person into being without exception, however that person's embryogenesis turns out.

So the first vocation from God that all of us experience is to be and to become a developing child. That has some important consequences. It means that when we watch a child grow we are witnessing vocation from God in action. When aunts and uncles, not having seen their nephew or niece for a few weeks, comment on how he or she has grown, they are testifying to God's purposes. So the role of parents and other family members in feeding, clothing and encouraging their

---

[6] Leroi, *Mutants*, pp. 50–1.

6

children as they develop is also a means of nurturing vocation. Similarly, when children examine their own bodies and learn to use them to explore the world, this can be thought of as a response to God's call. Play is similarly a vocational response to being embodied. Keith White wrote in his chapter in *Through the Eyes of a Child* that children taken to Wales found their surroundings to be one big adventure playground.[7] God's call is that we should from our earliest beginnings explore the creation and delight in it as God does. Conversely, the neglect or ill-treatment of children, which prevents them from flourishing, cuts directly across divine purpose.

Clearly, however, God's call to be and to become must also be extended to the entire unfolding of life within the creation, because embryonic development is not unique to humans. Leroi tells us that the early experiments that taught us about how embryos grow were conducted on creatures such as sea urchins, newts and toads. We can say that God as tenderly calls a robin into being within the egg, as the child you hold in your arms. The poet Christopher Smart saw in his cat's behaviour a 'worshipping' response to God's desire for him to grow as a cat.[8] What then is particular about God's call to human beings within the creation?

The image of God

Scripture offers us further pictures of God at work calling humans into being and here we learn more about why that call is not just a general exercise of divine will for the creation to be. An examination of the creation stories in Genesis is significant to our understanding of how God finds us worthy of calling into being, because although we are disposed to think of Adam and Eve as adults, principally because most paintings depict them as adult in form, it is perhaps better to think of them as 'new humans' just as any child is a new human. I will argue in Chapter 3 that the creation stories are analogous to a womb and birth experience for Adam and Eve. First, then, we are told something important about the new humans in relation to the creation.

---

[7] K. White, 'Creation', in A. Richards and P. Privett, *Through the Eyes of a Child* (London: Church House Publishing, 2009), pp. 44–67.

[8] C. Smart, 'Jubilate Agno', in M. Walsh, *Selected Poems of Christopher Smart* (Manchester: Carcanet Press, 1979).

> And God created the human in his image,
>> in the image of God He created him,
>> male and female He created them.
>
> And God blessed them, and God said to them, 'Be fruitful and multiply and fill the earth and conquer it, and hold sway over the fish of the sea and the fowl of the heavens and every beast that crawls upon the earth'. (Genesis 1.27–28)[9]

These verses of Scripture tell us that there is something significant about the creation of human beings which sets them apart from the creation of other living things. We see this in the way the account of the creation of human beings is set against the presence of animals, fish and birds, which are nonetheless part of God's 'good' creation. I suggest, however, that we can gain some insight into what it means to be made in the image of God if we continue with the theme of call. On this reading, the fact that a human being is made in the image of God means that we can respond to God's calling us into being and make a choice to be shaped by it. We see this implicitly in this passage, where the creation of human beings is immediately followed by God's speaking to the new humans. They are in relationship with him, they are given a task, they are entrusted with the rest of creation. Being made in the image of God offers us a particular kind of relationship which the nature of human intelligence, spiritual recognition and emotional response makes possible.

Another version of this is seen in chapter 2 of Genesis, which tells us even more about God's relation to humanity:

> then the Lord God fashioned the human, humus[10] from the soil, and blew into his nostrils the breath of life, and the human became a living creature . . . And the Lord God fashioned from the soil each beast of the field and each fowl of the heavens and brought each to the human to see what he would call it, and whatever the human called the living creature, that was its name . . . and the Lord God cast a deep slumber on the human, and he slept, and He took one of his ribs and closed over the flesh where it had been, and the Lord God built the rib He had taken from the human into a woman and He brought her to the human.

---

[9] R. Alter, *The Five Books of Moses* (New York: W. W. Norton, 2004), p. 19.

[10] Alter, *The Five Books of Moses*, p. 19, preserves the echo between the Hebrew words for 'man' and the ground from which he is taken.

And the human said:
'This one at last, bone of my bones
And flesh of my flesh,
This one shall be called Woman,
For from man was this one taken.'

We learn from this how intimately God is involved in the coming-to-be of a human being. God does not point from a celestial cloud, as in the Sistine Chapel, but is depicted more as a divine potter, guiding the raw material of the human's body into shape. God's hands are present in Adam's body and God's own breath is physically blown into the man's body to give him life. Further, God does not simply put more clay on his potter's wheel and mould another human, but is again intimately involved in the fashioning of the woman from the being of the man. If we put aside the long and sorry history of what Adam's rib has meant in the perception and treatment of women, we can see that this suggests that all human beings are not separate from one another, but connected, just as all children are born from their mothers' bodies, and that God is intimately and profoundly involved in that process. That point is reinforced by Adam's response to God's task. The living creatures are looked upon and named by Adam, he recognizes them as other to himself, and his naming confirms that difference. But the woman is recognized as his own flesh, a new individual, but standing in the same relationship to God. Both have experienced God's attention and involvement in their becoming in this personal and particular way.

It is important to realize that this creation story continues for us today. If we say that we are called into being by God, in a way that locates God's touch in our becoming, then God's breath is in our life, God's hands in the shaping and moulding of our flesh as our cells respond to the chemical signals to become human beings ready for birth. And further, as human beings, we should be conscious of that process in the becoming of others, recognizing them also as humans called into being by God and reflecting the image of God to us. We can say then that call and image go together and illuminate each other because they both emerge from the fundamental relationship between Creator and created that is at the heart of existence. Everyone is equally worthy of God's calling into being. We perhaps often become most aware of this at the birth of a child, when we finally see the 'living creature' that has journeyed to birth in the womb, recognizing her as 'flesh of my flesh' but also as a completely unique and never-before-seen individual, whom we name as one of us.

Jesus is also called into being

In Scripture, the Annunciation in Luke 1.26–56 is the visitation of the Angel Gabriel to the Virgin Mary to tell her that she has been chosen by God to bear Jesus: 'And now, you will conceive in your womb and bear a son, and you will name him Jesus'. Mary is understandably surprised to be told that she will become pregnant, asking, 'How can this be, since I am a virgin?' The angel replies: 'The Holy Spirit will come upon you, and the power of the Most High will overshadow you; therefore the child to be born will be holy; he will be called Son of God'.

This passage is for many people one of the touchstones of the Christian faith. The virgin birth is enshrined in the creeds and it sets Jesus apart from all other human beings who have ever lived. The conception and birth of Jesus are presented to us as miraculous and special because Jesus is the Son of God. For some people, including some theologians, the virgin birth is a theological problem rather than an explanation – a beautiful but unnecessary story obscuring rather than enhancing who Jesus really is.[11] The poet W. B. Yeats pronounced himself dissatisfied with the 'virgin womb and empty tomb' of Christianity precisely because these things spoke to him of absence and of the loss of the physical realities of birth and death.

I agree with Yeats in the sense that the foundational Christian belief that Jesus was born of a virgin can distract us from asking an important question: how exactly *did* Jesus become a human being in the womb of his mother? Theological thought about this can get tangled up with the matter of Mary's virginity. Did the miraculous conception mean that Mary was a kind of 'ark' for the Holy Child? How did she manage to give birth to him and still remain physically

---

[11] See, for example, J. Machen, *The Virgin Birth of Christ* (Cambridge: James Clarke & Co., repr. 1987); R. Gromacki, *The Virgin Birth: A Biblical Study of the Deity of Jesus Christ* (Grand Rapids, MI: Kregel Publications, 2002 [1974]); H. Turner, 'Expository Problems: the Virgin Birth', *The Expository Times* (October 1956) 68, pp. 12–17. An examination of the virgin birth as part of a complex of myth-narratives can be found in A. Welburn, *From a Virgin Womb: The Apocalypse of Adam and the Virgin Birth* (Leiden: Brill, 2008).

a virgin?[12] An important metaphor that was used was that Jesus came into the world like sunlight through glass: the light arrives but the glass is not affected. Contemporary biological understanding also made a difference. In St Augustine's time the assumption was that male sperm delivered the new person intact into the receptacle of the womb. For Jesus to have been born without original sin, the sperm needed to be taken out of the equation.

In view of what we now know about how children are conceived and grow in the womb, I think we should now ask what *else* can we learn from the annunciation in the Bible? Suppose that we understand that Mary's question is not just about whether she will get pregnant without having sex, but is also about how this particular pregnancy will happen in her womb. If we concentrate on the child that Mary is to bear then the angel's answer now tells us some very different things.

First of all, the angel's message tells us something which goes right back to the creation stories. God is intimately involved in the coming-to-be of human beings. In the case of Jesus, we are asked to understand that that intimate involvement takes God right into the process itself so that God experiences all of it, as we do. The Holy Spirit, which we know from Genesis is God's creative presence in the world, will be at the heart of the pregnancy – that reality of God's power and presence will be involved in the life and growth of Mary's child. To place that in the context of the Trinity: God calls Jesus into being; God responds to God's own self in becoming Jesus. That becoming incarnate is made possible by the creative will of the Holy Spirit. Yet all of this happens at the heart of God's own creation, in which the most natural thing in the world is a pregnancy and the birth of a new living creature.

Second, if we take from this that the Incarnation of Jesus occurs as the formation and growth of a child in a womb, then we can be sure that Jesus is really human just as we are, not a spirit, or God merely appearing in human form, but a person whose being was formed like us when God called him into being. Part of the problem for people trying to grasp the mystery of the Incarnation, is an attempt to make sense of it as a mind-boggling supernatural process,

---

[12] St Ambrose, *De institutione virginis et sanctae Mariae virginitate perpetua ad Eusebium*; F. Williams (trans.), *The Panarion of Epiphanius of Salamis* (Leiden: Brill, 1993); Lumen Gentium, ch. 8, available online at <www.vatican.va/archive/hist_councils/ii_vatican_council/documents/vat-ii_const_19641121_lumen-gentium_en.html>.

rather than recognizing that the angel's message offers us something about the heart of *being human* which we all have experienced and which we all share. The idea of God may sometimes feel very remote and otherworldly to us, but we are *connected* to Jesus. Remember too what Leroi tells us about the embryo burrowing into the womb. What we have learned through science about embryogenesis tells us that Mary was not just some vessel in which Jesus floated, or some fleshy incubator for the miraculous holy child, but that the unborn Jesus was deep inside her flesh and one with it, drawing from her all he needed at the biological level to become a child ready for birth, but also responsive to all the chemical signals and delicate organization that characterize the formation of the embryo in every other human person. As the embryo grows and develops in his mother's womb, Jesus is united not only with every other human person who must necessarily have grown in this way, but also to other living things in God's creation. Now when we hear St John's words 'What has come into being in him was life . . . And the Word became flesh and lived among us . . . full of grace and truth' (John 1.3–4, 14) we can have a greater insight into what that 'became flesh' actually means and have a greater and deeper appreciation for the body of Jesus, called into being and nurtured in the body of his mother.

So, if we concentrate on Jesus as child, born as one of us, called to be one of us, we discover something about the Incarnation which can be difficult to grasp from the theology of the creeds. What does it mean in reality? I think a child can tell us much better than I can.

I will steal a story from someone who used to be one of our local priests. Fr John McKeon used to tell this story just about every Christmas, usually at Midnight Mass. It goes like this.

When Fr John was a young priest in rural Ireland, many years ago now, he went into church on Christmas morning and went over to the Christmas nativity tableau on one side of the church. The star dangled over the stable, the shepherds gathered around adoringly accompanied by fat lambs, the ox and ass looked over the partitions of their stalls, and Mary and Joseph smiled beatifically into the manger filled with straw. But to Fr John's horror, they smiled at an empty space. Jesus was missing! Fr John panicked. In a few minutes people would be coming into church expecting to see the baby Jesus and all the other characters of the nativity story. Who could have stolen Jesus? Where was he?

Fr John went outside. There in the street were some young boys playing. And one of them was tearing up and down the street with the new wheelbarrow he got for Christmas that very morning. And there in the wheelbarrow, wrapped in a blanket, was the baby Jesus.

When asked why he had taken Jesus from the Nativity scene, the boy replied: 'You see, Father, I prayed to Jesus to get me a wheelbarrow for Christmas. And when he did I thought it was only fair that he should have the first ride in it!'

That story always got a laugh at Christmas Midnight. A gentle laugh at the funny ways of little children and their runaway imaginations. But to me that story has an extraordinary profundity. The boy prays to Jesus about his needs and desires, to a Jesus who is God and to whom a person can be intimately connected through prayer. But the boy also feels gratitude and joy on Christmas morning towards a Jesus who is divine but also human, a child. And that holy child doesn't want to be told about the wheelbarrow, he wants to *experience* it, to feel the excitement of being wheeled at speed down the street, to feel the air on his face and the giddy exhilaration that is also tinged with a bit of fear at the headlong rush of it, the fun of it. Jesus doesn't want to lie in his cradle and be goggled at; he wants to play and to be played with, and to delight with the other children in gifts given with love on Christmas morning. To me, that is the theology of the Incarnation in action, made simple, effective and real through a child playing in the street. As Proverbs 8.30–31 says:

> And I was by Him, an intimate,
> I was His delight day after day,
> before Him at all times,
> Playing in the world, His earth,
> And my delight with humankind.[13]

A double miracle

Sometimes readers of Scripture also forget that the annunciation of Jesus is only *part* of the angel's message. The other part is another pregnancy announcement: that Mary's cousin Elizabeth, who had not been able to get pregnant, was in fact carrying a child: 'For nothing will be impossible with God'. This is in fact the *first* pregnancy story

---

[13] R. Alter, *The Wisdom Books* (New York: W. W. Norton, 2010), p. 232.

in the Gospel of Luke, an annunciation to Zechariah, Elizabeth's husband, that she will become pregnant and bear a son who is to serve God. The two stories parallel and reinforce each other. In art, double stories like this were often visually represented as two halves of a painting or two separate parts of a scene which mirrored each other, so that people looking at them would see the stories shown side by side. It can be more difficult to remember that there are parallel stories if we don't read them together.

What happens next in Luke's Gospel is that Mary goes to visit Elizabeth, whose child will be John the Baptist.

> When Elizabeth heard Mary's greeting, the child leapt in her womb. And Elizabeth was filled with the Holy Spirit and exclaimed with a loud cry, 'Blessed are you among women, and blessed is the fruit of your womb. And why has this happened to me, that the mother of my Lord comes to me? For as soon as I heard the sound of your greeting, the child in my womb leapt for joy.' (Luke 1.39–44)

Why does the Gospel writer tell us this additional story? First, we are asked to imagine two pregnant women greeting each other. Each stands in the presence of a miracle, in the sense that neither thought that this circumstance could ever come about, but both now find that God has acted in their lives. Both believed that it was not possible to become pregnant, but here they are. They are both filled with the consciousness of God at work in their lives and are filled with gratitude and joy. Elizabeth's words become the basis of the 'Hail Mary . . .' prayer, but we may still forget that the context for the words is this powerful recognition and delight at the presence of God in the beginnings of us all. Mary and Elizabeth recognize that God is calling their children into being in the consciousness that their children have particular vocations from God. Mary knows that her son 'will be holy' and 'will be called Son of God'; Elizabeth knows too that her son is called to serve God. We know from the Gospel narratives that Jesus and John are closely associated and we see the outworking of the prophetic announcements about them when Jesus comes to John to be baptized, which, in the earliest Gospel, Mark, is the opening story (Mark 1.1–14). To my mind, there is a profound connection between the 'meeting' of the unborn children and the meeting at the Jordan in which Jesus submits to the ministrations of the Baptist.

Elizabeth feels her baby respond to Mary's voice and suggests that he reacts to the presence of Mary and Jesus; an *unborn child* is the first to respond to the presence of Jesus in the world. I think that this obscure little detail is extremely important and has been overlooked for far too long, perhaps because few of the traditional commentators have themselves directly experienced the movements of a foetus within them. These twin stories of Mary's and Elizabeth's pregnancies take us back to the essential goodness of creation. If an unborn child is capable of recognizing and responding to Jesus before either of them is born, then there is a goodness and rightness about their relationship to one another, as understood by Elizabeth, that refutes the idea that all human beings are separated from God by the fact of being. That is not to say that sin does not exist or that human beings do not have actively to change in order to experience the salvation offered by God, but it seems to me that this little moment offers a promise that unborn children are not irrevocably 'trapped in a second nature penetrated by sin'.[14] Rather the essential goodness of creation is present and recognizable in every new human who is called to be, and women who give birth to stillborn children or whose babies die before they can be baptized do not have to worry about what will happen to them.[15] Of course baptism of a seriously ill child can bring emotional and spiritual help to grieving parents, and the sacrament confirms the child's relationship before God, just as Jesus and John the Baptist met again and confirmed their vocations with and to one another. But if an unborn child has recognized Jesus, if the leaping in the womb is a 'Yes! I am here!', then as far as I am concerned the new or unborn child who has died can meet God face to face.[16]

---

[14] See M. Stortz, '"Where or When was your Servant Innocent?"' in M. Bunge, *The Child in Christian Thought* (Grand Rapids, MI: Eerdmans, 2001), p. 94.

[15] This matter troubled theologians such as St Augustine of Hippo who thought that if unborn children who had not been baptized were excluded from heaven because of their original sin, then they could only receive the lightest punishment; see the discussion in E. Ferguson, *Baptism in the Early Church: History, Theology, and Liturgy in the First Five Centuries* (Grand Rapids, MI: Eerdmans, 2009), p. 848. That Augustine was troubled by the outworkings of the theology of original sin is evident when he says: 'I cannot bring myself either to affirm or deny that they will share in the resurrection', D. Knowles (ed.), *Augustine: City of God* (Harmondsworth: Penguin, 1980), p. 1054.

[16] The Doctrine Commission of the Church of England couches the matter of ultimate destiny in terms of choosing God as the only source of life – or not. See *The Mystery of Salvation* (London: Church House Publishing, 1995), p. 199.

Some implications of God's calling us into being

Scripture, then, tells us some important things about how God calls every one of us, before we are born, just as Isaiah, Jeremiah and the psalmist tell us. We are called to form in the womb from the first cell of the fertilized egg to become the fully formed unborn child and God's call to us is deep within our being, just as a potter places his hands in the clay. We are called to be born and to take up our independent existence, to grow and to continue to live until our bodies fail us. Yet God's call never ceases; part of God's faithfulness is that God's relationship with us is never severed or broken off. What is started at conception continues for ever. We have also considered that we are made in God's image and that image is also what is called to be present before God and which informs our consciousness that God *is* calling us. Further, we share our physical life, our vocation from God, with Jesus the Incarnate Word, who has shared these remarkable beginnings with every human person. We have also learned that a spiritual understanding of the unborn child as desired by God and called by God to be an important part of God's creation is a message which is offered to all parents, not just mothers, and that such a spiritual recognition can bring both joy and awe.

Today, however, we live in strange times. Modern science has uncovered all these marvellous details about the development of the child in the womb, details which were not available to philosophers like Aristotle or theologians like St Thomas Aquinas or St Augustine when they pondered the becoming of the human child and worried about at what point the unborn child was possessed of a soul.[17] We also live in an era when we understand the precise hormonal mechanisms which make pregnancy possible, we can bring about artificial conception *in vitro*, we can freeze embryos and keep them for later use. We can transplant embryos into other wombs and we can manipulate embryos to make sure that the ones that begin to develop are free from genetic mutation or disease. We live in a time when women in the developed world can control their fertility and can even conceive children after their ovaries are destroyed or after

---

[17] According to Aristotle, 40 days after conception for males, 90 for females.

the menopause. We live in a time when women may choose whether to keep their pregnancies or terminate them.

We can see that while technology, and particularly the treatment of infertility, has given us extraordinary knowledge and control, the lessons I suggested we learn from Scripture are more difficult to hear in such an environment. But now we need to consider what those lessons mean in relation to what we now experience. We have said that God calls children into being. If that is true, then it is always true, no matter where or at what point the child is conceived. Moreover, if God calls all of us for ever, then there is never a point when God stops calling us to be; it doesn't make any difference if the embryo is developing in a Petri dish or lies deep frozen in liquid nitrogen. It doesn't make any difference if the embryo is in a womb which is not that of its biological mother. Nothing at all can change the fundamentals of the unborn child's existence before God. Furthermore, I have said that God is deeply and personally involved with the embryo's becoming, God's hands are dirty with the stuff of our being, so it follows that God cannot be shut out of the embryo's existence. Wherever the image of God is, there the presence of God is.

I have said that the growth and development of every human child reflects the delight of the Creator, and maybe we do hear some stories of great joy from the fertility clinics that can help couples have children, but there are many places in the world where the birth of a child is a source of fear, anxiety and disappointment. For example, in some cultures, it is important for economic and status reasons that a child must be a boy, and the birth of a girl is a failure, disappointment or worry. I was recently in South Korea standing before a statue of five fountains where you could pick whether you wanted to be blessed with long life, health, love, wealth or sons. In my westernized mental frame I didn't even recognize the word 'sons' and had to ask what it meant. In China, where many parents must pay a large fine if they have more than one child, another pregnancy can be financially devastating if not disastrous. In Africa, in those areas where many adults are infected with HIV, the birth of a child can be fraught with the fear that the child too will be infected. Even here in Europe, there are teenagers who fall pregnant as the result of abuse, women who are already struggling to bring up their children and do not know how they will feed another. All of these stories ask us to take thought about what kind of conditions need to exist for parents and *what has to change* so that they too can be glad of God's calling their children into being.

Ethical arguments about the beginning and end of life are often put in terms of the sanctity of human life, but when people think about this, they often think of that 'life' as a static, given quality of human personhood and it's sometimes difficult to understand what it means when we are talking about an embryo which is a few cells old. It helps, I think, to imagine that life as an unstoppable dynamic process of becoming. Unstoppable unless some biological defect causes it to die – or we stop it. Life is sacred because God's call to us to be is reflected in the response of our being to live. The frozen embryo cannot continue to develop, but it is still being called to do so and it never stops having the capacity to respond unless it dies. Thinking about it in this way reminds us that we can never treat embryos just as bits of tissue, or as commodities, or as of greater or lesser worth than other embryos.[18] Nor is God's call to be more significant in the lives of adults than it is in the lives of unborn children, infants or infirm elderly. Just because we are already living in the world does not automatically give our lives privilege over others in terms of God's call into being. Similarly, if as individuals or indeed as a society, we take decisions about abortion or discard embryos we do not need, then Christians need to face what is implied in those decisions: in the way I have framed it, it means we deliberately cut across God's loving call to the unborn. We interrupt a unique and personal vocation, irrespective of the number of weeks elapsed. I would suggest that we cannot destroy the unique knowledge of the individual which exists in the mind of God for ever, but we have to be responsible for what has happened to God's call when that vocation to be is terminated.

This further suggests that all adults should, as far as possible, be very aware of the need for personal responsibility in matters of sexual conduct: pregnancy can never be viewed lightly or as an inconvenience easily remedied. What we learn from Scripture is that our reproductive capacity and behaviour is a spiritual matter, deeply entangled with the purposes of God. This means that every pregnancy should be significant – and that human behaviour which leads to suffering,

---

[18] See, for example, B. McCarthy, 'Embryos Cannot be Reduced to Commodities', *The Guardian*, 11 February 2011.

cruelty towards and death among children cuts us off from what God desires for all human beings. It is also worth noting that in Scripture, while there are acts of infidelity which lead to pregnancies (e.g. David and Bathsheba in 2 Samuel 11), there are no 'accidents', 'mistakes' or 'unplanned pregnancies', because this kind of language is meaningless where people have no control over their biology. So it is worth considering what this difference between our lives now and the lives of the people of the Bible means. In western societies especially, we have more control and planning about how our children come into the world, but we have also created a world where the intimate becoming of a new person, whom God is calling into being, can be seen by us as a 'mistake'.

Some people are very aware of this. Consider, for example, Caitlin Moran's account of her decision to abort her child. Having wept countless tears for her first, miscarried pregnancy and having borne two healthy daughters, she finds herself unexpectedly pregnant:

> that really is it – there is nothing else that looks like a foetus. The curve of the spine, like an etiolated crescent moon. The astronaut helmet skull. The black, unblinking eyes, like a prawn.
>
> 'Oh my God,' I say, to the baby. 'Oh, you outrageous thing.' . . .
>
> . . . This kid is going to buck odds all his life: he'll break casinos, and befriend millionaires in the deli queue. He'll find gold the first time he pans the stream, and true love on the very day he decides he needs to settle down.
>
> 'I can't have you,' I tell him, sadly. 'The world will fall in if I have you.' . . .
>
> . . . I will do only one thing for this baby as quickly as I can, before it goes any further.[19]

Moran's account, which later spares us none of the pain and violence of the abortion itself, is interesting for this conversation with her unborn child. She broods over him, looking at how he is formed, how he is put together; she speaks to him, addresses him; she says he is 'the one I always wanted'; she imagines his life if he is born and comes to be all he is meant to be, it will be a charmed life, a happy life, a wonderful life. But then she says 'I can't have you' and decides that the most loving thing she can do for the baby is to abort him.

---

[19] C. Moran, *How to be a Woman* (London: Ebury Press, 2011), p. 270.

I find this account deeply challenging and I am still not quite sure what to make of it or how I feel about it, not least because in the mother's imagining of her unborn child's life, I cannot help but hear intimations of the divine vocation. On the one hand, Moran's grief for her lost child and love for her daughters is not in doubt, but at the same time to say 'I can't have you' to your own unborn child feels like the ultimate betrayal, even though she suggests it is still an act of love which means that she can bring up her daughters without guilt or regret. One thing this account makes absolutely clear, however, is that a healthy child who is called into being in a normal pregnancy *will be*, unless something is actively done to stop it. Doing nothing is not an option. So when we cut across the lives of children who are being called into being, we are faced with real responsibility and decision-taking: we have to be clear that we are saying 'I can't have you' with all that that refusal implies.[20] And at the heart of all such decisions for Christians, there is the matter of ultimately being face-to-face with God, with whom the life of the child, however brief, is forever intertwined.

How children recognize God's call

If children are called into being and recognize this vocation in the process of growth, development, exploration and play, then this biological 'yes!' can be complemented by a recognition of God's call and a positive response to it. Research by David Hay and Rebecca Nye discovered that children do often register a sense of relationship with God which can have an extraordinary effect on them. They called this 'relational consciousness' where children become aware that they are not alone in the universe but intimately connected to something at the heart of their being. The trouble is that these experiences are sometimes misinterpreted by adults, or, worse, reinterpreted by them, so that the child becomes confused or simply cuts off the experience, burying it, so that it does not have the chance to become a seed growing in the heart of the child's spiritual

---

[20] In *The Times* Magazine, 17 March 2012, Moran questions the way children can be called 'gifts': 'to a woman seeking an abortion, a baby is not a "gift" like a scented candle' (p. 5). However, children are precisely not static commodities and the issue of aborting a child is not at all like accepting or refusing a gift.

development. My favourite example, from their book *The Spirit of the Child*, comes from a six-year-old called John:

'Well once I went um . . . in the night and I saw this bishopy kind of alien. I said, "Who are you?" And he said, "I am the Holy Spirit". I did think he was the Holy Spirit.'[21]

John told his mother about this amazing experience, but she contradicted his account, telling him that the Holy Spirit looks like a ball of fire, even though he confided to Rebecca that he did really feel that it was a genuine experience and that he was aware of 'the Holy Spirit in me'. This story reminds us that we should expect the unexpected in relation to how children become aware of God's presence in their lives and how they react to it. Making assumptions about how God works, or what God's presence looks, feels or sounds like, can in fact be counterproductive and interfere with how children say 'yes!' to God. But parents and teachers and all who are charged with the care and nurture of children are important and necessary in helping children realize that God's call to them is present in their lives. We can learn about how that works from Scripture.

Scripture has a famous example of God calling a child and the child responding to that call, but what is not sometimes understood is that the story of the call to Samuel has important parallels with the story of Jesus in the Temple in Luke 2, so it is worth considering both these stories against each other. If we do that, the story of Samuel helps us learn important things about Jesus' own vocation. We can start with what we learn from 1 Samuel.

Samuel is not just any child. His life is profoundly intertwined with dedication to God. His mother, Hannah, had no children and prayed to God that she might conceive. Her promise is that she will repay God for hearing her prayer by promising her child to God's service. Eli, the priest, sees her praying desperately to the Lord, but thinks she is drunk, and she has to explain to him what she was doing. When Samuel is born it is Eli who oversees the consecration of the child and Hannah's song, which becomes a poetic template for Mary's Magnificat, is one of joy and gratitude for her pregnancy and her child. She keeps her promise and as a child dedicated to God, Samuel is left in Eli's service.

---

[21] D. Hay and R. Nye, *The Spirit of the Child* (London: HarperCollins [Fount], 1998), p. 102.

The context matters. The child is recognized as a blessing and that is recognized by placing the child in the heart of the love and worship of God and in a life of service to God. This suggests that how we view our children and how we bring them up matters, if they are to recognize their calling and know it for what it is. It matters that we are properly thankful for our children. It matters that we hold them before God. After telling us about Samuel's birth and dedication, the story moves on to the dramatic account of Samuel's call.

Tradition suggests that Samuel was about twelve years old at the time, the same age given for Jesus when he remained in the Temple.[22] This is significant because boys of this age were considered at the point of making moral and ethical decisions for themselves and preparing for entry into the adult community.

> Now the boy Samuel was ministering to the LORD under Eli. The word of the LORD was rare in those days; visions were not widespread.
>
> At that time Eli, whose eyesight had begun to grow dim so that he could not see, was lying down in his room; the lamp of God had not yet gone out, and Samuel was lying down in the temple of the LORD, where the ark of God was. Then the LORD called, 'Samuel! Samuel!' and he said, 'Here I am!' and ran to Eli, and said, 'Here I am, for you called me.' But he said, 'I did not call; lie down again.' So he went and lay down. The LORD called again, 'Samuel!' Samuel got up and went to Eli, and said, 'Here I am, for you called me.' But he said, 'I did not call, my son; lie down again.' Now Samuel did not yet know the LORD, and the word of the LORD had not yet been revealed to him. The LORD called Samuel again, a third time. And he got up and went to Eli, and said, 'Here I am, for you called me.' Then Eli perceived that the LORD was calling the boy. Therefore Eli said to Samuel, 'Go, lie down; and if he calls you, you shall say, "Speak, LORD, for your servant is listening."' So Samuel went and lay down in his place.
>
> Now the LORD came and stood there, calling as before, 'Samuel! Samuel!' And Samuel said, 'Speak, for your servant is listening.' Then the LORD said to Samuel, 'See, I am about to do something in Israel that will make both ears of anyone who hears of it tingle. On that day I will fulfil against Eli all that I have spoken concerning his house, from beginning to end. For I have told him that I am about to punish

---

[22] For example this age is given in Josephus, *Antiquities*, Book 5 (10.4).

his house for ever, for the iniquity that he knew, because his sons were blaspheming God, and he did not restrain them. Therefore I swear to the house of Eli that the iniquity of Eli's house shall not be expiated by sacrifice or offering for ever.'

Samuel lay there until morning; then he opened the doors of the house of the LORD. Samuel was afraid to tell the vision to Eli. But Eli called Samuel and said, 'Samuel, my son.' He said, 'Here I am.' Eli said, 'What was it that he told you? Do not hide it from me. May God do so to you and more also, if you hide anything from me of all that he told you.' So Samuel told him everything and hid nothing from him. Then he said, 'It is the LORD; let him do what seems good to him.'

As Samuel grew up, the LORD was with him and let none of his words fall to the ground. And all Israel from Dan to Beer-sheba knew that Samuel was a trustworthy prophet of the LORD. The LORD continued to appear at Shiloh, for the LORD revealed himself to Samuel at Shiloh by the word of the LORD. (1 Samuel 3.1–21)

This story has some important features. First, the beginning of the story suggests that there is a dearth of an active sense of God's presence and that it is precious when it comes. Although Samuel is brought up close to the Presence and at the heart of the worshipping community, yet visions and prophetic activity have died down. So when Samuel lies down to sleep he does not expect to encounter God's call.[23] Second, the call to Samuel comes in an entirely natural form. It is not a huge supernatural event but something simple and guaranteed not to cause fear. Samuel becomes aware that someone is calling him by name. He naturally assumes that it is Eli and obediently responds, only to be told that it was not Eli who spoke. Further, there is a deeper point in the Hebrew of a movement from the sense of being *summoned* to a sense of calling as *invitation*. Samuel believes that he is obeying a summons from Eli, but it needs Eli to recognize that something else is going on in the child's life and to suggest to him how to hear the call and how to respond to it. Similarly, when Samuel has heard God's word and commission, he is afraid to reveal it. Eli again must help the child fulfil his task. This creates the context for a life lived in God's presence. The response of Samuel to God's call nurtures in him the prophetic vocation.

---

[23] I use 'encounter' because it is not clear that this is just something Samuel hears.

But the drama of the story invites us to consider something else – what was it like for the child to encounter God in this way? This is, after all, Yahweh, whose Holy of Holies Eli and Samuel serve, yet it is a personal, intimate voice that speaks Samuel's name and rouses him from sleep. There is also a complex interpersonal dynamic, since Eli is Samuel's master and teacher, but God's call to Samuel separates him from this relationship and makes him a mirror of God's feeling towards Eli. God's call to a child then may be intimate but it is not sugar-coated. The child is trusted with speech which will create tensions and awkwardness.

The opening of Luke's Gospel strongly echoes the story of Samuel. Mary, who as yet has no child, is told that she will give birth and praises God using similar language to the song of Hannah. We are told of Jesus' circumcision and the prophecies surrounding him as a special child of God.

> Now every year his parents went to Jerusalem for the festival of the Passover. And when he was twelve years old, they went up as usual for the festival. When the festival was ended and they started to return, the boy Jesus stayed behind in Jerusalem, but his parents did not know it. Assuming that he was in the group of travellers, they went a day's journey. Then they started to look for him among their relatives and friends. When they did not find him, they returned to Jerusalem to search for him. After three days they found him in the temple, sitting among the teachers, listening to them and asking them questions. And all who heard him were amazed at his understanding and his answers. When his parents saw him they were astonished; and his mother said to him, 'Child, why have you treated us like this? Look, your father and I have been searching for you in great anxiety.' He said to them, 'Why were you searching for me? Did you not know that I must be in my Father's house?' But they did not understand what he said to them. Then he went down with them and came to Nazareth, and was obedient to them. His mother treasured all these things in her heart.
>
> And Jesus increased in wisdom and in years, and in divine and human favour. (Luke 2.41–52)

We are told that Jesus was about twelve years old when this event happened. The family, along with others in their community, travel to Jerusalem for Passover, but when they leave Jesus stays behind. His parents are worried when he is not found and go back to Jerusalem to look for him. They find him in the Temple listening to the teachers there.

As with the story of Samuel, there is a tipping point in the child Jesus' life in which the place of God in the child's life becomes something which must be examined and embraced. Teachers are particularly important in this process of discernment and allow a space in which questions like 'Who am I?' and 'What does God want of me?' become paramount, even to the point of keeping Jesus in Jerusalem, though he should be with his parents. Similarly, Samuel needs Eli to explain how to hear, understand and relate to God's call. In both cases, the child runs the risk of antagonizing his elders: Samuel has words of judgement to relay to Eli; Jesus upsets his parents. Yet these are also important moments of growth and decision and are decisive in who both Samuel and Jesus are to become. Luke makes this explicit: Jesus grew physically, but also spiritually. He was obedient to his parents but also to God as the call in him became explicit.

Many commentators on the Gospel of Luke make much of Jesus' words to his parents. The exact translation of verse 49 is problematic, but two things emerge forcefully – Jesus' attempt to get over to his parents the sense of impulse or urge that kept him there, and the reference to 'my Father', as a specific and real orientation to God. William Barclay writes: 'Here we have the story of the day when Jesus discovered who he was'.[24] Some commentators think this offers a little picture of the humanity of Jesus, a stroppy child answering back after being told off, and that the words 'my Father' come as a slap in the face to Mary and Joseph. I suspect, however, that there is an edge of awe and wonder in the words 'my Father' which Jesus is anxious to share with his parents. It is, if you like, an overt sharing of God's place in Jesus' life: a testimony. Jesus is not setting himself against his parents, but describing his own understanding of the path in which they have nurtured him. We are told that this is not some beginning of a violation against the commandment to honour one's father and mother, but a settling into the devoted life, and this is reinforced by our being told that Mary treasures these things in her heart.

---

[24] W. Barclay, *The Gospel of Luke* (Edinburgh: Saint Andrew's Press, 2001 [1953]), p. 36.

So I think whatever this event in doing in the Gospel of Luke, and whatever the author of Luke-Acts means us to understand by this ending of the birth and childhood narrative of Jesus with this story, the words 'my Father' at this juncture are pivotal. We can see that this particular and intimate relationship becomes a mainstay of Jesus' teaching and in speaking about his relationship with God to others. Indeed the Lord's Prayer begins with 'Our Father'. The understanding reached in the Temple, from contemplating Scripture and his Jewish tradition, becomes a backbone of what will be Jesus' teaching and public ministry and will underline key decisions in Jesus' adult life.

These passages of Scripture ask us to think about what goes on in any child's life which sows seeds of purpose and vocation and they remind us as parents, teachers and carers that we should enable the spiritual growth of children which may be discerned not just when the children are sitting at our feet asking questions and acquiring knowledge but also when they appear to be testing the boundaries or saying and doing things we don't really understand. Rebecca Nye, for instance, tells the story of some children who were mucking about in church, throwing paper aeroplanes, but whose aeroplanes turned out also to be a testing of a gospel message.[25] These boys were supposed to be part of a children's group, but all they did was make aeroplanes out of the paper provided. The problem was that the congregation expected to see a result – an outcome from the children's time spent in the group. Yet from this activity Rebecca Nye learned two things – first that the boys were enjoying a time just to be themselves, in fact experiencing the Sabbath as it was meant to be experienced without having to account for their labours to others, and second, that making the aeroplanes gave them something to experiment with. After exploring the resurrection story, those same aeroplanes became a means of testing what crucifixion and resurrection means. When Rebecca picked up a discarded aeroplane she found it had been made 'with Jesus' body hanging from the dark cross, and the empty cross on the other [side] in brilliant shiny, white card'.[26] The point here is that children's spirituality can cut

---

[25] R. Nye, 'Spirituality', in P. Privett and A. Richards (eds), *Through the Eyes of a Child* (London: Church House Publishing, 2009), pp. 68–84.

[26] Nye, 'Spirituality', p. 70.

across our adult expectations and the unexpected and the trivial can be places in which children discover important truths about who God is for them and in their lives.

These stories underline the importance of teachers who are sensitive to children's spiritual needs and provide them with the discernment they need to explore what possibilities God is putting before them. Further, such teachers, helpers and role models in the child's life need to allow the child space to test that what he or she experiences is real and meaningful. Eli allows Samuel a physical and mental space to explore the call; Jesus puts both time and space between himself and his parents in order to explore the teaching in the Temple. But once that exploration has taken place, the child still needs the nurture and protection of adults to fulfil that new understanding of what God's call means for them. It is important that Jesus goes away with his parents and is obedient to them. The recognition of call and relationship to God is not a sealed contract but a seed which needs to grow.

These stories have some positive implications for how we treat our own children. In the first place, God is with them; we do not have to do anything in particular for God's vocation to become real in our children's lives. That having been said, creating a context in which it is natural to believe that God is a real and loving presence in the lives of human beings creates a spiritual space in which children can more easily become aware of their spiritual growth. Conversely, we have to realize that there are many children whose lives do not contain these opportunities for spiritual growth, and for whom sometimes even the beginnings of spiritual exploration are shut out or shut down so that they may become simply unspoken or fossilized, perhaps for the rest of the children's lives. In an increasingly secularized society it may be that this sense of a denied or lost spirituality becomes more and more common.

For example, Rebecca Nye describes a conversation with another child, Joanna:

> speaking about her imaginary garden, Joanna said she liked to play at being the Queen of this garden in which she enjoyed magnanimous power to bring things back to life. In her imaginary garden it was always sunny and peaceful. She explained that her garden was a retreat

when her noisy, and sometimes gloomy home life got on top of her. She was aware that going to her garden was helpful, and sensed that for her this kind of thing had transforming potential.[27]

Joanna's garden becomes a glimpsed experience of the life into which God calls children. For her the garden becomes an expression of hopefulness, happiness, peace and potential. Yet for many children that glimpse may be all they have. That issue is the one I want to consider next.

I also want to hang on to the confidence that Scripture shows us that God finds children worthy of calling. Further, we discover that God is not waiting for children to 'grow up' or to reach a particular stage in development, rather that there is a point at which children come to realize that their experiences and explorations mean something for their future, when they can say 'here I am' in a consciousness of God's presence in their lives. How they make sense of that call and work out its meaning for them depends on their environment and their own willingness and capacity to explore. Yet that also means that we may not like the *results* very much at all. This matter of commission will be explored in Chapter 3.

Some questions for reflection

- What early memories do you have which had an impact on your later life?
- Where do you see children offering evidence of spiritual awareness and growth?
- What kinds of thing do you think hinder children from becoming aware of God's call?
- Where might you recognize God's calling to be in the growth and development of children?

Activity

What *one* thing could you change in your own situation which would allow children more space to hear and respond to God's call?

---

[27] R. Nye, *Children's Spirituality: What it is and Why it Matters* (London: Church House Publishing, 2009), p. 37.

2

God finds children worthy of life and salvation

'Grow . . .'

Before we get to the way God offers commission to children, I think we need to start with something much more basic. The first matter to be clear about in the issue of children's 'salvation' is that children should have a life. There is an important principle stamped within the Scriptures: that God does not want any child to die. Children are called into being, and it is in being delivered into life that they can have the space and the time for them to come to know who God is. In his vision of the world God wants to see, in the new Jerusalem, one of the writers of Isaiah declares: 'No more shall there be in it an infant that lives but a few days . . . They shall not labour in vain, or bear children for calamity; for they shall be offspring blessed by the LORD' (Isaiah 65.20, 23). This section of Isaiah makes a bold statement about God's purpose and intention for a redeemed creation. There will be no more tears, and no child will have to die. Raymond Fung calls this the Isaiah Agenda, God's vision for the way the world should be.[1]

We may find this rather confusing, part of the struggle with words and meanings, because, in the world of the Bible, children do die, *all the time*. In examining the demographics of families even in the time of Jesus, Reidar Aasgaard has shown that women needed to bear at least five children to have any chance of successfully raising two of them to adulthood.[2] Sometimes, even successfully raising a child could end suddenly in bloody violence. Who can forget the outpouring of David's grief when he receives news of his son

---

[1] R. Fung, *The Isaiah Vision: An Ecumenical Strategy for Congregational Evangelism* (Geneva: WCC Publications, 1992), p. 2.

[2] R. Aasgaard, *My Beloved Brothers and Sisters: Christian Siblingship in Paul* (London: T&T Clark, 2004), p. 38.

Absalom's murder: 'Oh my son Absalom, my son, my son Absalom! Would that I had died instead of you, O Absalom, my son, my son!' (2 Samuel 18.33).[3]

In the world far from Eden and the tree of life, children die from disease, famine and warfare in a world at mercy of weather, sickness and struggles for power and territory. Sadly, in many parts of the world today, the same conditions exist. The biblical world is a world without sophisticated medicine and prey to occupational violence. Strange, random violence can suddenly erupt from the pages of the Bible. For example, in 2 Kings 2.23–25, a group of young people often translated 'children' or 'small boys' jeer at the prophet Elisha's appearance, 'Go up bald head!' and he curses them. In the next moment, it seems, two she-bears come out of the woods and rip and maul them.[4] In fighting between different groups, children were often immediate victims of bloody conquest. Even the psalmist imagines a violent death for the children of Babylonian captors:

> Daughter of Babylon the despoiler,
> happy who pays you back in kind,
> for what you did to us.
> Happy who seizes and smashes
> your infants against the rock.[5]
>
> (Psalm 137.8–9)

Robert Alter comments that there can be no moral justification offered for this 'bloodcurdling curse' but asks readers to consider the circumstances of the powerless exiles whose lives have been looted and their families massacred. Alter brings out the sheer violence of the curse, seizing and smashing children's brains out. On the other hand, Lamentations brings out in vivid detail the sufferings which Israel's children have endured: 'The tongue of the infant sticks to the roof of its mouth for thirst; the children beg for food, but no one gives them anything . . . The hands of compassionate women have boiled their own children; they became their food' (Lamentations

---

[3] Absalom is described as an extraordinarily beautiful young man, a lad (2 Samuel 14.25). When he is killed he is involved in a battle against David's forces.

[4] Perhaps we are meant to remember the warning in Leviticus 26.22 that those who are disobedient towards God (and God's prophet?) can expect such violence to happen: 'I will let loose wild animals against you, and they shall bereave you of your children'.

[5] R. Alter, *The Book of Psalms: A Translation with Commentary* (New York: W. W. Norton, 2007), p. 475.

4.4, 10). God is also implicated in the circumstances of children's deaths; they are collateral damage in the way a sinful world implodes. But the essential point even in a world imagined to be full of divine wrath and judgement is that God does not *want* any of these children to die. To discover what this tells us about God's relationship with children, I want to contrast the God of divine wrath, whose judgement falls upon his people, with three biblical metaphors: the weeping woman, the courageous midwife and the she-bear.

The weeping woman

This violence of the ancient world is nowhere to my mind more vividly realized than on the Sagrada Familia cathedral in Barcelona, designed by the architect Antoni Gaudi. On the exterior there is a sculpture of a Roman soldier, his right arm holding a metal sword which protrudes wickedly from the building. A mother desperately kneels before him, grabbing his arm, while his left hand, held high above his head, holds a small baby well out of her reach. What is about to happen is crystal clear, for the corpses of other tiny, naked children lie littered at his feet, their lifeless bodies draped over the stone lip. When I first saw this sculptural depiction of the Massacre of the Innocents (Matthew 2.16) it reduced me to tears, not least because in the kneeling woman who tries to stay the hand of human murderers against her children, I saw the suffering of God who sees those newly called into being laid waste because of human fear, pride and ambition.

The voice of Rachel, weeping for her children (Jeremiah 31.15 and quoted in Matthew 2.18), is to my mind also the voice of God, lamenting the departure of the ways of the world from the divine vision. In fact, in the Jeremiah passage, that lamentation and refusal to be comforted is also set within a promise of restoration and comfort: 'there is hope for your future, says the LORD: your children shall come back to their own country' (Jeremiah 31.17). Children die every day, but God who has called them into being, regrets and laments the loss of that potential to flourish and grow. At the same time it is God's desire for human beings that children should be saved and that tears should be dried. So we should expect to see God at work against the human forces of destruction and death. And so we do; and we do it, of course, through and in Jesus.

With that in mind, the massacre of the innocents in the Gospel of Matthew achieves a new focus. God comes to be with us, but not as some avenging angel or great superhero, but as a vulnerable child who could himself so easily die. The Gospel concentrates that risk for us and Herod's determination to root out and kill those children who could be a threat to him is a terrifying background for the safety of the newborn Jesus. Even *God's* son is not automatically protected from the harsh and evil ways of the world. He is born into a place and time where another wants to murder him, and he will leave it when finally other murdering influences get their way.[6] Yet God's salvation never ceases to be operative. The writer of Matthew's Gospel tells us that Joseph, his heart open to God, receives a warning about the risk to the child and takes Jesus away from harm. But this means that others are not so lucky. Yet God is not satisfied with the knowledge that Jesus has escaped; God's pain for all those others who have died remains. The voice of the bereaved mother who has lost her child cannot be silenced and nor can the fierce promise of God that in a reconciled world, tears will be remembered and restoration take place.

The courageous midwives

Another important metaphor may be found in the story of the courageous midwives in Exodus 1. Even in slavery in Egypt, the Israelites increase in number. They are fruitful and multiply. In response to this, Pharaoh demands that the midwives, in whose hands the lives or deaths of babies lie, should kill the baby boys. At the point where God's call to children to be becomes the beginning of their lives as independent beings, at the beginning of a journey to growth and flourishing, human power and ambition demands that those lives be cut short. But the midwives lie to Pharaoh, choosing life over death, and insisting to him that Hebrew women give birth before the midwives get near them. The

---

[6] I suspect that the brief comment in Matthew about Jesus going to be by himself when told of the death of John the Baptist (Matthew 14.13) shows Jesus acknowledging and grieving for the way the murderous powers have overtaken the person with whom his own life has been intertwined and perhaps seeing in it a prefiguration of his own end. If this is true, then what Jesus does next, curing the sick and feeding the crowd, shows the divine determination to overcome the forces of death with compassion, nurturing and healing.

great Jewish commentator Rashi tells us that the text of this story is shot through with allusions to nurture, life-giving, and giving the newborns food and water.[7] This commentary about the midwives also provides an interesting parallel with the Massacre of the Innocents in that it tells us that Pharaoh was supposed to have been told that a boy would be born among the Israelites who would grow up to save them. Moses, like Jesus, is initially in grave danger. I think, then, that the courageous midwives also embody for us something of the desire of God to save, not just in the sense of preserving life against the forces of destruction, but in enabling, protecting and nurturing.

The she-bear

But elsewhere in Scripture, God is not just the weeping mother whose struggle is to try to stay the hand of the murderer, is not just to be found at work in the midwives who go up against the power of the Pharaoh, but is the passionate mother, who is roused against those who deprive children of life. In Marcia Bunge's book *The Child in the Bible*, in a chapter called 'Vulnerable Children, Divine Passion and Human Obligation', Walter Brueggemann discovers an important metaphor in three places in the Hebrew Scriptures: 1 Samuel 17.8, Proverbs 17.12 and Hosea 13.8, which carry the words 'like a she-bear robbed of her cubs'.[8] Brueggemann tells us that this metaphor helps us to think about the divine passion of God which is like a roused she-bear, who will stop at nothing to seek out human injustice and work tirelessly in creation to care for the little ones. This is a matter of God's nurture, God's passionate love and God's justice. The fact that all these metaphors are female may also be instructive. Charlotte Perkins Gilman suggests that anthropologically, 'male' religion may be more oriented towards death, especially sacrifice, but that filtered through a female lens religion becomes birth-based and life-giving, it is 'necessarily and essentially altruistic, a forgetting of oneself for the good of the child, and tends to develop naturally into love and labor for the widening

---

[7] The Complete Jewish Bible with Rashi Commentary, Exodus 1 online at <www.chabad.org/library/bible_cdo/aid/9862/showrashi/true>. Rashi, Rabbi Shlomo Itzhaki, was a French rabbi in the medieval period.

[8] W. Brueggemann, 'Vulnerable Children, Divine Passion and Human Obligation', in M. Bunge, *The Child in the Bible* (Grand Rapids, MI: Eerdmans, 2008), pp. 399–422.

range of family, state and world'.[9] If this is true, then it is interesting that even in the world of the death-dealing judging God who acts on *the world as it is*, the Bible insists on giving us images of a God who desires that the world should be life-affirming and life-giving – *the world as it should be*. So if we look upon a happy, cared-for, flourishing child, we see a glimpse of the world as God intends it.

So this is how we discover that God does not want any child to die, by finding God as a weeping woman, as a midwife and as a she-bear roused to passion at the hurt done to her cubs. These female metaphors give a sense of the life-bearing and life-giving. What will God's salvation look like? The writer in Isaiah 11.8 includes this salvation in his vision of the messianic age: in addition to peace and tranquillity a little child will lead the wild animals without fear of harm and 'the nursing child shall play over the hole of the asp, and the weaned child shall put its hand on the adder's den' (Isaiah 11.8). The world, which is so dangerous to children and in which so many die, will be a place of safety and salvation, where children can play, grow and flourish. In this vision especially, children are found worthy of God's salvation.

What does this say to us today?

I have suggested that we find three images or metaphors for the way God finds children worthy of salvation: God as weeping mother, God as midwife and God as roused she-bear. How do these metaphors of action towards and about children help us think about how we behave towards and on behalf of children today?

The image of the weeping mother can be a powerful one, because it does not have to mean hopeless passivity in the face of male aggression. The weeping woman in Picasso's *Guernica*, holding her dead child in her arms, does not bow her head in despair but sends up a howl towards heaven that cannot be ignored. The tears of women and of God are powerful enough to rock governments and provoke change. For example, the Mothers of the Plaza de Mayo are a protest movement who have been campaigning for thirty-five years. These are women who have lost their children through government abductions

9 Charlotte Perkins Gilman, 'Female God Language in a Jewish Context', in C. Christ and J. Plaskow (eds), *Womanspirit Rising: A Feminist Reader in Religion* (San Francisco: Harper & Row, 1979), p. 172, quoted in D. Hampson, *Theology and Feminism* (Oxford: Blackwell, 1990), p. 140.

and long to be reunited with the 'Disappeared'. The Mothers are known by their trademark white headscarves, which symbolize the children they have lost. The Mothers (and Grandmothers) continue to demand that they are told what happened to their children.

'They touched the most sacred thing a woman can lose, a son. I was 45 years old when they took Alejandro. I'm almost 80 now and I don't know what happened to him. I've been waiting all this time,' says Ms Almeida. 'Of course we know they are dead, but politically they are still "disappeared-detainees" until those who did this tell us what they did with them.'[10]

The Mothers refuse to go away. They refuse to forget the Disappeared. Like the dead child at the heart of the Judgement of Solomon, they bring what is wrong with the world into the light of public scrutiny. In doing so, they align themselves with God's purposes. Similarly, Winnie Johnson, who died in 2012, never gave up the pressure to find the remains of her son Keith Bennett, aged 12, murdered by Ian Brady and Myra Hindley in 1965. Mrs Johnson's single-minded desire was to give him a proper burial. 'I'll do anything, go anywhere for him,' she said of her dead son. 'As long as I know one day, I'll be grateful. I hope he's found before I am dead. All I want out of life is to find him and bury him. I just wish he is found before I go.'[11]

We have also seen Doreen Lawrence, the mother of the murdered teenager Stephen Lawrence, found a charitable trust in his name and work tirelessly for better community relations and against hate crime so that other children might not lose their lives through racist violence. The artist Chris Ofili painted a portrait of a weeping black woman, called *No Woman, No Cry* (1998), which shows an image of Stephen Lawrence in each of the woman's tears.[12] This extraordinary painting shows to us the power of the weeping woman to carry the memory of the dead child and to change the world for others.

In the work of other children's charities and organizations, we also see dedicated people working as 'midwives' to give children a chance. There are many such important charities, dealing with issues such as childhood diseases, poverty, abuse, trafficking and exploitation.

---

[10] V. Hernandez, 'Argentine Mothers Mark 35 Years Marching for Justice', BBC News 29 April 2012, online at <www.bbc.co.uk/news/world-latin-america-17847134>.

[11] See <www.telegraph.co.uk/news/obituaries/9486186/Winnie-Johnson.html>.

[12] The painting was bought by the Tate Gallery in London in 1999.

To mention just a couple of important charities in the UK: the National Society for the Prevention of Cruelty to Children (NSPCC) works to stop children experiencing pain and suffering at the hands of others.[13] It also provides Childline, a service which allows children to talk about and get help for problems such as bullying, exam pressure and physical abuse.[14] The Children's Society campaigns for ways to give children a chance: finding ways to make runaways safe from the people who would prey on them; supporting child carers so that they can have a life of their own and a break from their burdens; and finding practical ways to give children in poverty the life essentials they need.[15] Barnardo's works to change the lives of vulnerable children and by research, projects and campaigning, fights to give those children a better future.[16] These organizations resist the powers of evil and injustice which can blight children's lives and work to create a space in which every child's potential can be fulfilled.

We also see contemporary examples of parents as roused she-bears. In these cases, parents are not just keeping memories alive by their tears, but using the tools of media and communication to advocate for change. We may think of Sara Payne, the mother of Sarah Payne who was murdered, aged eight, in 2000. We may also think of Kate McCann and her husband, Gerry, whose daughter Madeleine disappeared in 2007. Mrs Payne has since become a 'victims' champion' and independent voice for the victims of crime. She has also campaigned for 'Sarah's Law', legislation to help parents protect their children against paedophiles. The McCanns have campaigned ever since their daughter's disappearance to find out what happened to her, using books, television, interviews and media articles to keep their daughter's face before the public eye. Despite controversy about methods and objectives, it is clear notwithstanding that the determination of these mothers breaks open institutional processes, overcomes bureaucratic wrangling and places the lost child constantly and tirelessly before the eyes of all of us.

Yet today, as in the world of the Bible, children do still die. Despite our individualized and often selfish society, we do recognize the

---

[13] <www.nspcc.org.uk>.
[14] <www.childline.org.uk>.
[15] <www.childrenssociety.org.uk>.
[16] <www.barnardos.org.uk>.

outrage against the way the world is when a child dies needlessly. While that is true for every child who dies from famine, illness or poverty, some cases become embedded in our imagination, especially when they happen on our own doorstep. The cases of Victoria Climbié[17] and Baby Peter[18] in the British news media have been particularly acute. Their deaths at the hands of people who were supposed to be caring for them and the agencies whose job is to identify children at risk have come under the spotlight in a way that indicts us all. We perhaps understand instinctively that such acts undermine the human social order, but more than this, these deaths go up against what God wants for the lives of children. It is not just human social fabric but divine purpose that is thwarted and destroyed by the pain and suffering of such children.

What does God want to happen then? Where does Scripture tell us about how children are threatened by death and destruction, but yet found worthy of salvation?

Giving children a chance: instances of salvation

Moses in the bulrushes

> And a man from the house of Levi went and took a Levite daughter, and the woman conceived and bore a son, and she saw that he was goodly, and she hid him for three months. And when she could no longer hide him, she took a wicker ark for him and caulked it with resin and pitch and placed the child in it and placed it in the reeds by the banks of the Nile. And his sister stationed herself at a distance to see what would be done to him. And Pharaoh's daughter came down to bathe in the Nile, her maidens walking along the Nile. And she saw the ark amidst the reeds and sent her slavegirl and took it. And she opened it up and saw the child, and, look, it was a lad weeping. And she pitied him and said, 'This is one of the children of the Hebrews.' And his sister said to Pharaoh's daughter, 'Shall I go and summon a nursing woman from the Hebrews that she may

---

[17] Victoria Climbié was an eight-year-old girl who was tortured and murdered by those looking after her in 2000. After their conviction, a public inquiry was conducted which led to changes in child protection policy.

[18] The death of Baby Peter was remitted to justice and the result was the sacking of Sharon Shoesmith as head of social services, as well as the conviction of the mother and her boyfriend for the abuse of the child.

suckle the child for you?' And Pharaoh's daughter said to her, 'Go'. And the girl went and summoned the child's mother. And Pharaoh's daughter said to her, 'Carry away this child and suckle him for me, and I myself will pay your wages.' And the woman took the child and suckled him. And the child grew, and she brought him to Pharaoh's daughter and he became a son to her, and she called his name Moses, 'For from the water I drew him out.'[19]   (Exodus 2.1–10)

We have seen already that the story of Moses arises from the context of the courageous midwives who defy Pharaoh's death-dealing decree 'Every boy that is born . . . you shall throw into the Nile' (Exodus 1.22). They ensure that Hebrew baby boys have a safe delivery. Just as those babies are drawn safely from the amniotic waters of the womb, so Moses is drawn from the water to safety, despite being marked for death. This familiar story once again has a background in God's promises to those whom he calls into being. The word for Moses' basket, his 'ark', is the same as the word for Noah's ark, the vehicle through which human-kind was kept safe from the Flood. The ark is the mode of salvation and new beginning in relationship with God. Against that cosmic background, there is the folktale-like story of peril and salvation.

This story is woven around the motives and behaviour of a series of dedicated women who together conspire and work to preserve Moses' life. His mother makes his 'ark' and hides him in it. Then she lets him go. His sister watches out and over him. Pharaoh's daughter finds Moses and takes him in, drawing his mother and sister into the future of his nurture. His mother continues to feed and care for him, and Pharaoh's daughter, adopting him into her life, keeps him safe from the death sentence.

This is a good illustration of how children are found worthy of salvation in Scripture. Pharaoh's daughter knows that Moses is one of the Hebrew children and that he lives in the shadow of death, but she responds to his need and offers preservation not destruction. People of different faiths, different cultures, different social standing and dif-ferent backgrounds all work together to save Moses. This personal story also shadows the larger story of the Israelites. They too are under threat and need a story of salvation. By following God, the people 'multiplied' thus harking back to God's command to the primordial

---

[19] Alter, *The Five Books of Moses*, pp. 312–13.

humans. It is no surprise that Moses' commission is to lead the people to safety through the water. We progress from the midwives safely delivering babies, to Moses, through God's help, delivering an entire people from the waters of the Red Sea to new life on the other side: the intimacy of birth, the calling to be of the new human, is scaled up to the birth of a nation, called to be God's chosen and to be ethically holy.

God's salvation then is linked in this story to the idea of being drawn from water. The text indeed suggests that there is an etymological link between Moses' name and the sense of being drawn from water (or perhaps actively drawing from water). This metaphor, distilled into both the name and person of Moses, labels him as one who embodies the salvation God wants for us all. To enter into the water is a desperate peril, but the Lord delivers. Consequently, at every act of baptism, the child or other baptized person enters the water, dies and is raised to new life, experiencing God's salvation for himself and finding a world of new possibilities with God on the other side.

The story of Moses shows us a child under a death sentence, but Scripture also shows us children who are actually dead or brought to the point of death in sacrifice. What does God want for them? If we struggle a bit more with some of the Bible's difficult passages we can discover more about God's intention and the ways in which God desires that children be saved. Then we can see whether what we have found out gives us pointers for the way in which children are worthy of life and salvation in our world today.

The judgement of Solomon

The judgement of Solomon (1 Kings 3.16–28) is a famous biblical story which has two children at its very heart, another of the twin or parallel narratives in which the lives of two children are intertwined. Two 'prostitutes' come to King Solomon and tell him their stories. Both were pregnant and both gave birth. Both were living in the same house. Both were nursing their sons when, it is alleged, one of the women accidentally smothered her child and killed him by lying on him. The mother of the dead child then switched the dead body of her child with the living one of the other woman. The other woman denies this and both women argue before the king that the remaining child is theirs.

Having listened to all this, King Solomon's judgement is to call for a sword and propose to cut the child in two, thus killing it but offering an equal 'share' of the child to each of the women. The mother of the dead child agrees, thus equalizing the status of the other woman with her own, but the living child's mother asks the king not to do it, to let the other woman have the child as long as the child remains alive. By examining these responses, the king realizes that the mother who begs to spare the child is the 'true' mother and in the light of this 'truth', mother and son can be reunited.

Some feminist commentators are troubled by this narrative. Solomon, the very icon of male power, arrives at truth by the threat of violence and a show of force. The 'wrong' woman responds to this male violence by submitting to it; the true mother is revealed by responding to her biology; 'the two women "judged", then, are defined not only by utterances, but by the bodily process by which those utterances are determined to be attached'.[20] Rabbinic commentators offer us a number of other ways into this story. One asks us to consider that the women were not prostitutes but widows who needed living children to protect them from levirate marriage, that is, having to marry the brothers of their dead husbands in order to have children within the family. Another suggests that the women are actually supernatural beings come to test Solomon and make his wisdom known to the people. When he says 'she is his mother' he has spoken God's truth. On this reading, this is not then just a human story, but a glimpse into the ways of God with human beings.

Recently, I was at an exhibition in the British Museum which featured a painting of this biblical story by an unknown Flemish artist. What was striking about the painting was that the living child, squirming, held by his leg by a man with a sword, was right at the bottom of the painting. By contrast, the dead child was featured at the very centre of the canvas, at Solomon's feet, grey and lifeless. The eye was inexorably drawn to him. So I would like to get away from the struggle with what the adults are about and turn this story on its head by asking what we can make out about what God wants for the lives of children.

First, what we know about the children is that they are completely vulnerable. Their lives and deaths are in the hands of the adults who look after them or who can decide their fate. There is nothing the

---

[20] M. Ashe, 'Abortion of Narrative: A Reading of the Judgement of Solomon', *Yale Journal of Law and Feminism* 4.81 (1991–2), p. 86.

newly born child can do except be the passive recipient of the ways of adults and this is driven home by the image of the woman smothering her child during the night. This vulnerability is heightened by the fact that the fate of the surviving child is driven by the dead child who has (presumably) accidentally been killed by his mother. The story appears to be about a living child, a surviving child, but the *dead* child is the precursor and the driver for the whole event. The loss of that child, the child who should not have died, is an equally compelling story within the heart of the narrative.

There is a bereaved mother and a mother whose child has been abducted, both suffering and both clutching at the same lifeline – a live child to nurse and nurture. For both those women, the meaning of their pregnancy and birth experiences lies in being called the mother of the child. But for only one of them, that narrative of motherhood is 'truth' and it is this which Solomon has to decide. But what is he deciding? On the one hand he decides where the surviving child has the best chance to flourish and grow and, on the other hand, he refuses to allow the other mother to replace her dead child, whose life had meaning and who must be mourned. Consequently, Solomon decides the 'truth' by testing which the women will choose – the life of the child or the death of the child on the one hand, or, put another way, the chance for the child to be nurtured and to flourish, even at personal cost and loss. 'Justice' is therefore for the surviving child's continuing life and for the life of a child who should not have died, and not just for the women.

The dead child's mother has still lost her child. The dead child is still dead. Only the living child, who was threatened with death at the point of the sword, has been redeemed by a divine discernment: God's wisdom in Solomon's decision. Yet we can find that the story tells us clearly that God does not want any child to die; the dead child should still be at the centre of the scene as having worth and significance. He is to be remembered, and through his death the living child is saved and must now have the chance to grow. This tells us that because God does not want any child to die, when a child *does* die, that should make us redouble our efforts to build a world in which children can flourish as God desires.

Let us now turn to the fates of two more children, not infants, but somewhat older.

Ishmael and Isaac

And Abraham rose early in the morning and took bread and a skin of water and gave them to Hagar, placing them on her shoulder, and he gave her the child, and sent her away, and she went wandering through the wilderness of Beersheba. And when the water in the skin was gone, she flung the child under one of the bushes and went off and sat down at a distance, a bowshot away, for she thought, 'Let me not see when the child dies.' And she sat at a distance and raised her voice and wept. And God heard the voice of the lad and God's messenger called out from the heavens and said to her, 'What troubles you, Hagar? Fear not, for God has heard the lad's voice where he is.

Rise, lift up the lad
And hold him by the hand,
For a great nation will I make him.'

And God opened her eyes and she saw a well of water, and she went and filled the skin with water and gave to the lad to drink. And God was with the lad, and he grew up and dwelled in the wilderness, and he became a seasoned bowman.   (Genesis 21.14–20)[21]

Many people familiar with Bible stories remember the horror of the near-sacrifice of Isaac, but forget that in the book of Genesis, Abraham has *two* sons, both of which come into mortal peril. Robert Alter, in translating the five books of Moses, points out the linguistic similarities between the two stories, suggesting that the writer of this part of Genesis wants the fates of the two boys to be intertwined and considered together.[22]

The first story is a terrible drama of banishment. Abraham, having fathered a child (Ishmael) by his slave-woman Hagar, now has a legitimate heir (Isaac) by his wife, Sarah. Sarah tells Abraham to get rid of Hagar and her child, so Abraham sends her away with a small supply of food and drink. Whether this is a temporary measure, a permanent one, or Hagar is expected to find shelter elsewhere becomes a side issue, for Hagar and Ishmael, who is probably an adolescent at this time, run out of water. Hagar is grief-stricken, not just for herself but for her son, and does not want to watch her child die. But it is not Hagar's tears that God specifically responds

---

[21] Alter, *The Five Books of Moses*, pp. 104–5.
[22] For example, 'Abraham rose early in the morning', Genesis 21.14; 22.3.

to, but Ishmael's cries. God then sends a message of comfort to Hagar, urging her to find courage and not to give up. So it is Hagar who finds water with which to save herself and Ishmael and finds the means to care for and raise Ishmael in the wilderness to become the 'seasoned bowman' with the skills to survive in that tough environment and to grow into his adult life.

This part of the story tells us that God hears the cries of imperilled and dying children 'where they are'. And God responds. In addition, in calling him into being, God has made a promise about Ishmael and that promise holds for ever. The strength of the unbroken promise and the cries of the child bring about God's saving response. Alter points out that the etymology of Ishmael's name is 'God will hear' and here is the proof of the power of that name. Further, the word 'na'ar', translated by Alter as 'lad', has behind it a sense of affection and intimacy; God's tenderness towards the suffering boy. Terence Fretheim says of this story that

> God's will for the child is evident in several ways ... that the child live, that the child no longer be deprived, and, more generally, that he thrive in a life of stability. This is a massive testimony to God as one who cares for all children, not just those who are members of the chosen line. Out in the middle of nowhere, God is with this excluded child, a child excluded by good, religious people; God provides for him through means that are available quite apart from a religious community. The text is testimony that God is present and active out and about in neglected parts of the world, providing for the health and welfare of children, both insider and outsider.[23]

We need to hold on to that important observation.

In the judgement of Solomon, we saw that God's desire reaches through to the story of a dead child and the tragedy of his death, which allows a ruling that gives life to the survivor by finding the right person to care for him. In the wilderness we find God at work, hearing the cry of a dying child and enabling his mother to nurture him to adulthood. This means that God's desire for each one of us is also poured out upon those who will care for us and enable us to fulfil the commission that God offers us. Parents and all those

---

[23] T. Fretheim, 'God was with the Boy', in M. Bunge, *The Child in the Bible* (Grand Rapids, MI: Eerdmans, 2008), p. 13.

entrusted with the care of children really matter and, through this story, we see that God will give parents and carers the tools they need even when it all seems impossible or hopeless. In view of this, what on earth are we to make of the parallel story in Genesis about Ishmael's brother? What are we to make of a parent who goes out to kill his own beloved son?

The sacrifice of Isaac

In the Jerusalem Chamber at Westminster Abbey is a large tapestry depicting an unusual subject: the circumcision of Isaac. We know from the Bible that the rite of circumcision for males in the tradition of Israel was an important ritual event, bringing new male children into the community and physically marking them according to God's covenant command to Abraham (Genesis 17.9–14). Circumcision takes place on the eighth day after birth and the circumcision of Jesus is itself recorded in the Gospels.

Yet this tapestry is remarkable in another way. The child is tiny, naked and vulnerable and over him the elders lean with their vener-able beards; more significantly, the knife is poised ready to remove the *bris*, the foreskin, and make Isaac formally one of their own (see Genesis 21.4). What we see is the child and the point of the knife poised over him. It is a reminder that all male children of the com-munity were subject to this important ritual – they underwent a symbolic death, a cutting and a shedding of blood; they passed through an ordeal and emerged as part of their community. So significant is this ritual that circumcision is still a significant rite in modern Jewish tradition and circumcision as an anthropological sign of passing into the community, or through adolescence is still practised in many cultures. The circumcision of Jesus is twinned with a recognition of his status in the Gospels and is attendant with the recognition of God's salvation in the Song of Simeon and the praise of Anna. Later Christian traditions turned his foreskin into a holy relic which itself could work miracles. St Helena is supposed to have worn it like an invisible ring.

The circumcision of Isaac as represented in the tapestry is surely intended as a visual reminder of a story which to my mind is one of the most perplexing and difficult in the Hebrew Scriptures. According to Genesis 22.1–19 God himself asks Abraham for a sacrifice, but not the usual animal offering, a sacrifice of his own son. This will require Abraham to take Isaac, his longed for and beloved child, ritually slaughter him with a knife and burn his body on an altar. Abraham, obedient to the word of God, takes his son and wood for the sacrifice and sets out to do as the Lord commands.

In those ancient times, human sacrifice was practised by many communities. The gods were immense, dangerous and demanding and human life desperately precarious. Human sacrifice met various needs: offering up life to preserve life, to appease angry or jealous gods, or to atone for destructive sin. In particular, the association of the firstborn with the gods of fertility meant that such children should be made over to the gods in order to ensure fertility of crops and enable the people to survive and grow. In Exodus 13, we are told that God said to Moses that the firstborn of both human beings and animals should be made over to God. However, in the community of Israel, there was a move away from human sacrifice to the substitution of animals for human children. Consequently, we can read the story of the sacrifice of Isaac against this background, as it answers the question: what does God want?

The story is dramatic, but perhaps we should remember that God has discovered Ishmael in the wilderness and already saved him. Robert Alter tells us that we should spend more time thinking about verse 2, which he translates as 'your son, your only one, whom you love, Isaac'. Alter tells us that we should listen to Rashi, who spells it out for us as a dialogue. First Abraham speaks and then God, in turn:

> He [Abraham] said to Him, 'I have two sons.' He [God] said to him, 'Your only one.' He said to Him, 'This one is the only son of his mother, and that one is the only son of his mother.' He said to him, 'Whom you love.' He said to Him, 'I love them both.' He said to him, 'Isaac.'[24]

Rashi helps me to sense in this verse a driving home to Abraham of what Abraham has done to *Ishmael*, whom God has saved, although Abraham does not know this. In Rashi's commentary, Abraham maintains that he (still) has two sons, but in this interpretation

---

[24] The Complete Jewish Bible with Rashi Commentary, Genesis 22.2 online at <www.chabad.org/library/bible_cdo/aid/8217/showrashi/true>. Also see Alter, *The Five Books of Moses*, p. 108.

God presses on Abraham that he has now effectively chosen Isaac over Ishmael, even though God's promise extends to them both. Abraham is suddenly faced with the possibility that he may lose both his sons. He has already sacrificed one to the wilderness, now God is demanding from him the other. Even though, culturally, Isaac takes precedence as the legitimate heir, this is not an excuse. God hears the cries even of the illegitimate and abandoned.

In Rashi's dialogue, Ishmael is still in Abraham's mind. But Isaac is a precious child, born to Sarah when she believed she was too old and barren to have children of her own. All of Abraham's hopes now centre upon Isaac and Abraham's belief is that God will use him to found a great nation. Is it guilt that brings Abraham to submit and obey God's demand that he sacrifice Isaac? Does he feel that it is a fit punishment for Sarah, who encouraged Ishmael's coming into the world, yet who has now encouraged his expulsion from his family group? This is a critical moment, because if the demand for appeasement and sacrifice overcomes the promise of hope, then Israel will founder.[25]

Nonetheless, the story sees Abraham setting off in obedience to an apparently bloodthirsty, jealous and angry God. The drama continues. Isaac knows that something worrying is going on and asks his father where the animal for the slaughter is. Abraham builds the altar, ties up his child and lays him upon the altar then raises the knife to kill him. At the last moment, a voice from heaven tells him to stay his hand and let the child go. This moment is often seen as a test of faith, but another way of looking at it is that Abraham is forced to confront what he has done to Ishmael, even though he did not murder him himself. If Ishmael is out of sight and out of mind, raising his knife to kill Isaac would surely represent to him in graphic terms what his son might have suffered. But God does not want *any* child to die. Abraham miraculously finds a ram that is caught in the thorns and the ram is sacrificed instead. God's voice promises that fertility will continue and the community will be blessed.

---

[25] Human sacrifice is not unknown in the world of the Hebrew Scriptures. In 2 Kings 3.27, the king of Moab, in desperate straits and about to lose to the Israelites, sacrifices his firstborn son as a burnt offering for victory. In 2 Kings 16.3, Ahaz is condemned for making 'his son pass through fire'. In addition the giving over of the firstborn to God in recognition of God's role in continuing fertility was a powerful idea. See, for example, Exodus 22.29.

The narrative offers us at one level an intimate psychodrama teaching us that blood sacrifice is no longer necessary and animals can be substituted as offerings to God. The purpose and utility of such offerings will continue – fertility will be maintained as well as the right relationship with God. Yet at another level, there is another message: God does not want children to be hurt and killed by their parents. The story does not just offer us the changing mental view of Abraham whose dialogue and relationship with God is the driving force behind the narrative. Rather we also hear the anxious voice of the child as he realizes that he is somehow at the heart of the preparations for and the process of sacrifice. What does God want? The question is not only a tribal one, a ritualistic one, but also a personal one. The answer is that the child must be protected, spared, and that human fears, desires, even the good of the community, must not be visited on the child. Consecration to God now means something else, something other than the giving over of life in death. While we may baulk at the implied trauma Isaac must have undergone, being taken out into the desert, tied up and placed on an altar of sacrifice, the other side of this traumatic journey is the message that it is never too late to turn back. Even at the point of death and under the power of a driving psychological force, both of Abraham's sons must be freed and restored. The drama of death becomes a drama of salvation. The radical nature of this change is underlined by the divine edict from heaven to spare the child.

Jephthah's daughter

I can't leave the ransom of Isaac, however, without acknowledging a young person who was perhaps not so fortunate. In Judges 11.29–40, we learn that Jephthah, a person who has experienced rejection like Ishmael, and who like him has become a warrior in the wilderness, a kind of outlaw, is called back to fight against the tribal enemies of Israel. Jephthah, fighting his way through all these enemies, makes a vow, a bargain with God. If he is successful against the Ammonites he will offer as a burnt offering whatever he first sees coming out of his house on his return. In the text, the vow is cast as if Jephthah is thinking of something male and because human and animal habitation was all part of the same complex, it is possible that Jephthah thought he would be more likely to see an animal suitable for a sacrifice than a human being. But it is his young daughter who comes to meet the victor 'with timbrels and with dancing'. Jephthah is stuck. He has made a solemn vow which he cannot break. Though stricken with grief for his only child, he accedes to her request to be given two months to mourn her virginity. When she returns he fulfils his vow. In fact some commentators argue that we are not actually told that Jephthah killed her and that 'did with her according to the vow he had made' could mean that she remained unmarried and given to God, a Nazirite.[26]

I don't think we can overlook the possibility that she was actually sacrificed, but even if not, it is clear from the time of mourning that what was lost, sacrificed to the needs of power and victory, is some kind of important potential in the young person. The writer of the text wants us to realize the extent of this loss, with its picture of the lively dancing girl whose desire for life and love is cut off by her father: 'she had never slept with a man'.[27] It raises the question, does God *want* a young person to die powerless in exchange for victorious battle, or want a person to give up marriage and family against her personal choice?

In answering this question it seems particularly significant to me that the girl, in obedience to her father, says 'do to me according to what has gone out of your mouth' (v. 36). Human words can mean death to others or trap innocent people in places they do not want to be. God's word, however, creates and gives life. I don't therefore find it surprising that in the following chapter, Judges 12, we get a powerful contrast with Jephthah's words, when the angel of the Lord announces to the wife of Manoah that she will conceive and bear a son.[28] Here Manoah prepares a burnt offering of animals and sees the angel of the annunciation go up in the flame. Terrified, Manoah thinks that they will die for having encountered God, but his wife

---

[26] See Numbers 6.1–21. Nazirites were set apart or separated out in order to devote themselves to God's service. Such people made vows to God and proved their promises by avoiding all grape products, not cutting their hair (hence Samson's famous hair) until the appropriate ritual and taking care to remain ritually pure.

[27] Phyllis Trible uses this story as one of her 'texts of terror' highlighting the darkness and fear of parts of the Bible in which women are hurt, abused or killed. See P. Trible, *Texts of Terror: Literary-Feminist Readings of Biblical Narratives* (Minneapolis: Fortress Press, 1984).

[28] Perhaps we might also remember here Mary's words to the angel at the Annunciation, 'let it be with me according to your word'.

says that God would not have said all those things to them if he had meant anything but life. The word of God gives life and brings salvation into the world; the word of human beings who think only of temporal and violent ends, power and victory against others, deals death. (Her son, incidentally, is Samson.)

Putting the story of Jephthah's daughter against the promise to Manoah shows what God really wants for the lives of children: life and deliverance from evil. But human beings still manage to put children and young people into situations where they cannot flourish and may die.

What can we learn from these stories about what God wants for children today? One thing which particularly stands out is that these narratives remind us to consider how important parents and other family members are in the nurture and care of children who are called by God to grow and to flourish. Yet all kinds of terrible pressures afflict those who care for children: pressures from family, from culture, pressures from society, pressures from economic hardship, bereavement or suffering. So while God does not want any child to die, the salvation of children in *this* world also depends on adult carers themselves having the space and opportunities to make sure children can be protected, encouraged, nurtured and allowed to flourish.

Parental pressure in today's society

Sadly, those who care for children are not always able to cope. Studying these stories from Scripture makes me pay more attention to questions about what kind of pressures lead parents to abandon children. What economic circumstances, accidental and shameful pregnancies, fear, despair or indifference lead parents to leave their children on the doorsteps of orphanages, or hospitals? What we learn from the stories of Isaac and Ishmael is that we need to pay attention to how these things happen and what combinations of circumstance bring such situations about. What role do *we* have in the abandonment of Ishmael today? Every child who is starving, or drinking filthy water, or is kicked out of his home or simply ignored because another child is favoured more, all of these children are heard by God. God does not want them to die, either physically, mentally or spiritually. When we look at our Isaacs, who, though loved and cherished, suddenly get sick, or have accidents; when we sit at their bedside and pray that they must get better, must get through this, we glimpse the passion of God for *every* child, the ones we never consider the rest of the time.

Another important consideration from the story of the brothers, Isaac and Ishmael, and the story of Jephthah's daughter, is to remember that despite the revelation of God's will that Isaac be spared, there are too many children around us today who are sacrificed daily. Even if we no longer have blood offerings, children are still sacrificed in other ways by adults with driving psychological motives: adults who have been abused often abuse their own children in turn; children are worked to death; children are sacrificed for economic motives, or left to die of hunger or disease. Yet, even at the point of death, the divine voice commands us that these children should be spared, brought back and the evils of the world which lead children to their deaths must be challenged. Children are worthy of salvation and our task is to find alternatives, just as Abraham, finally, did.

There are other sorts of pressures too, equally insidious perhaps and which flourish in the opposite kind of circumstance. In wealthy western society parents come under pressure to see children as accessories, whose clothes, toys, accomplishments or abilities have to be honed to reflect the status, power or fashion awareness of the parents. Such pressures lead to the creation of children as mini-adults, sexualized before they are grown; or children whose gifts and interests are suppressed in favour of becoming clones of their successful parents. Such children, who may seem superficially to have everything, may also be in need of salvation.

What does parenting have to do with God's finding children worthy of salvation?

The matter of how adult interests can suppress or distort the space children need in order to grow is exemplified by another case which, like the one brought before Solomon, asked a judge to decide on what should happen to a child. Like Archbishop Rowan Williams, whose letter to Lulu I mentioned in the Introduction, the judge in this case decided to write directly to the child at the heart of the dispute. The matter of the dispute was whether the child could be baptized.

Dear C,

It must seem rather strange for me to write to you when we have never met but I have heard a lot about you from your parents and it has been my job to make an important decision about your future.

Sometimes parents simply cannot agree on what is best for their child but they can't both be right. Your father thinks it is right for you to be baptised as a Christian now. Your mother wants you to wait until you are older so they have asked me to decide for them. That is my job.

I have listened to everything your mother and father have wanted to say to me about this and also to what you wanted to tell me. You have done that by speaking to the Cafcass lady[29] and she has passed on to me what you said to her. That has made my job much easier and I want to thank you for telling me so clearly why you want to be baptised now. It is important for me to know how you feel.

My job is to decide simply what is best for you and I have decided that the best thing for you is that you are allowed to start your baptism classes as soon as they can be arranged and that you are baptised as a Christian as soon as your Minister feels you are ready.

Being baptised does not mean that you give up your Jewish heritage. That will always be part of you and I hope that you will continue to learn more about that heritage and about your mother's faith. Even after you are baptised you are still free to change your mind about your faith later when you are older. Finally, and this is the most important thing, both your mother and father will carry on loving you just as much whatever happens about your baptism.

I understand that the past few months have been a difficult time for you but that is over now and the decision is made. I send you my very best wishes for the future.

Yours sincerely,

Judge John Platt[30]

This letter was written to a child 'C' as part of a judgement at Romford County Court in Essex. C was aged ten and a half and was the subject of a disagreement between her divorced parents. Both her

---

[29] Cafcass stands for Children and Family Court Advisory and Support Service. In this case, the 'Cafcass lady' is a Family Court Adviser who gives an informed opinion about what is best for the child.

[30] Judgement of Judge John Platt in the Romford County Court online at <www.bailii.org/ew/cases/Misc/2012/15.html>.

parents and all her grandparents were Jewish, but it was reported that they did not practise their religion in any meaningful way. C however came into contact with the 'New Wine' Christian movement and as a result of her experiences, said that she wanted to be baptized as a Christian. Her father agreed, but her mother objected, and brought a 'prohibited steps' order against her father to prevent C doing anything about becoming a Christian until she was sixteen. The judge ruled that C should not be confirmed in the Christian Church until she was sixteen, but that her mother should not prevent C from going to baptism classes or from being baptized. He pointed out to C in his letter that her Jewish heritage was important and could not be taken away from her and that if she wanted, she could still change her mind about what religious tradition she wanted to follow at a later stage.

In August 2012, the journalist Joshua Rozenberg wrote an article in *The Guardian* newspaper entitled 'Suffer the Little Children to Come Unto Me'[31] commenting on this case. His view was that the judge had acted wisely and sensitively in listening to and acting on C's spiritual needs. But then he comments that the issue could have been avoided by giving the family's two children a proper spiritual framework:

> You may well think that it would have been in the child's best interests if she could have remained entirely secular, as she had been for the first eight years of her life. Let her choose when she grows up, some might say. But the wider lesson from this case is that it is surely desirable to give one's children some sort of ethical structure to cling on to as they grow up – beyond teaching them obedience to their parents and the difference between right and wrong, as these two children were properly taught. It may be one of the world's established religions, provided it is taught in a loving, measured way.

I've heard many parents tell me that they have decided not to baptize their children, but to let them 'make their own minds up' when they get older. While this seems on the surface to be a non-intrusive liberal kind of parenting which is designed to give the child freedom to choose, sometimes that very argument is a turning away from

---

[31] J. Rozenberg, 'Suffer the Little Children to Come Unto Me', *The Guardian*, 8 August 2012.

parental decision-making and passing the buck and the burden to the child, so that the parents don't have to be bothered with it. Even some parents who have brought their children to baptism have since told me that they did not intend to do anything about bringing up their children as Christians despite the promises they made, but to let the child choose at some 'point' in the future when, they imagine, religious decisions have to be made. C's mother made some of this argument, suggesting that C was too young to make such a decision.

Rozenberg, however, suggests that bringing a child up in a faith tradition provides an important and necessary structure. It is not a matter of forcing religion down a child's throat, but offering beliefs and practice in 'a loving measured way'. This, he suggests, would avoid a child, already suffering from the fact of her parents' divorce, finding her needs met by the first intense spiritual experience she encountered. This is an interesting question about the spiritual needs and life of children and the role of parents in making sure those needs are met. In this case, the judge offered something which had been missing from the child's life: an acknowledgement of her spiritual life and journey; listening to her views and wishes; opening up the immediate decision to encourage her to explore her cultural and spiritual heritage; and, perhaps most importantly, offering her a freedom to change her mind.

I am interested in this view of the 'conversion' at the heart of the dispute and I want to think further about how the judge's letter to the child reflects on what we might say about how God finds children worthy of salvation. Here again is a judgement on the future of a child, which highlights the critical role of parents in providing their children with room to grow. With increasing incidence of divorce and remarriage, judgements about where children should live and when they should see absent parents continue to require the wisdom of Solomon. It seems to me that all these matters impact on the idea of salvation, which I want to argue is not a fixed 'thing' to be attained (in say, the language of 'winning' a soul for Christ) but a much more fluid nexus of influences and explorations in which a child can question, decide and undecide as she grows. In the Romford case, that exploration was made available through baptism class. Salvation then is intimately related to met needs, growth and flourishing.

In Judge Platt's judgement he wants the Jewish parents and their daughter's Christian teachers to work together to help the child experience for herself what God's salvation might mean for her. The Jewish mother, who fears for her child, is asked to trust others who do not come from her own background. She is asked to trust that they will nurture her daughter and include her in deciding what is to happen to her. She is invited to watch but not to interfere. Just as Moses did not forget his own heritage and what it meant in Pharaoh's household, so C is encouraged by the judge not to forget her religious origins and what they might mean for her later as she grows up. The judgement therefore offers her a way to experience God's salvation. That salvation might mean a way of coping with the consequences of divorce, it might mean finding new friends, it might mean an entirely new and exciting religious experience. Whatever it means, the journey will take her to a place where she will be drawn from water, and know for herself God's promise to hear the cries of lost children and to bring about new life. This is a God who loves and nurtures as a parent loves a child, even when the children stray:

> When Israel was a child, I loved him,
> And out of Egypt I called my son.
> The more I called them,
> The more they went from me;
> They kept sacrificing to the Baals,
> And offering incense to idols.
> Yet it was I who taught Ephraim to walk,
> I took them up in my arms;
> But they did not know that I healed them.
> I led them with cords of human kindness,
> With bands of love.
> I was to them like those
> Who lift infants to their cheeks.
> I bent down to them and fed them ...
> My heart recoils within me;
> My compassion grows warm and tender.
>
> (Hosea 11.1–4, 8–9)

From all that we have looked at in how God finds children worthy of life and salvation we can extract the following principles:

- a principle of remembering and recovery for all those children whom God does not want to die but still did and still do;
- a principle of justice for those whose lives fall short of what God wants for them;
- a principle of growth and flourishing for the lives of children.

What does this last principle mean? That there should be both adequate space and time in children's lives for them to answer God's call fully. Children have physical needs – food, water, fresh air, security and health. Children need adequate opportunity to play and explore, access to education which provides them with the tools they need to grow, and finally space for spiritual exploration.

Parents, then, have a remarkable and testing responsibility for ensuring that God's desire for the nurture of children comes to fulfilment. We see this set out not just in Hosea but in the words relating to the childhood of Jesus, that the child grows into what God wants for him and is found to be full of grace and truth. What happens after that we will look at later.

Some questions for reflection

- What do you think about Judge Platt's letter to C? Do you agree with his judgement?
- What would you have done in Solomon's place to find out who was the mother of the disputed child?
- In what ways do you think we can help people whose children have died?
- What do you think are the signs that children are living a healthy, happy life?

Activity

- What is going on in your own life, church or community, which helps children to live life fully? What *one* thing might you be able to do to improve the lives of children in your area? The children's charities mentioned in this chapter might give you some ideas.

3

God finds children worthy of commission

'Act . . .'

In this chapter, following on from the example of C wanting to explore baptism, I want to look at how children arrive at a place where they are able to say 'yes!' to God's calling.

There's a game I used to play with my two children when they were primary school age. My job was to be a pompous and arrogant customer in a restaurant ordering fish and chips or apple pie and ice cream. One of my sons took my order with exaggerated politeness, writing it all down on a piece of paper, while the other made a huge amount of noise in the 'kitchen' banging pots and pans and expressing exasperation in (inexplicably) a faux-Spanish accent.

I never got what I ordered. What I got was platefuls of things the children did not like to eat but which I continued to feed them at mealtimes as part of what I considered a healthy diet. 'You've got BROCCOLI!' they'd scream, slapping imaginary steaming lumps of green stuff on to my plate, 'AND SMELLY FISH.' And they'd look on sternly while I affected disgust and horror and demanded to complain to the manager. Great fun was had by all.

I was reminded of this game when I saw an advertisement on television for a programme fronted by Chris Tarrant in which children were allowed to do adult jobs. The purpose of the programme was comedy – watching children say and do funny things. I never actually saw this programme but I was very struck by one of the trailers in which a child was allowed to run a funfair attraction. The attraction was one of those where you try to win an impossible game in the hope of winning a big prize. In this case, the big prize was a large cuddly shark.

Although it was supposed to be almost impossible to win a big prize, the child was unable to send people away disappointed after playing his game, so as time went on more and more people were seen carrying sharks. Asked about this, the boy said, 'Some people have got sharks . . . but don't tell my dad.' Faced with adult responsibility, the child's generosity overcame the 'rules'.

It seems to me that behind the laughter in both these stories there is something serious going on at the heart of it all – a message to us as adults that we can miss because we're laughing at the children and thinking how cute they are. My children were teaching me a lesson about what it feels to be the subject of adult power and what it is like to have things forced on you that you don't want, even if it is 'good' for you. The child at the funfair was sending a message about justice and love overcoming the 'rules' which stack the odds in some people's favour against others.

In Scripture, when children respond to God's call, we can't just laugh at them or dismiss them. Children are found worthy of commission, not because they're cute, but because they have something very particular through which something of God comes to others. I don't want to use phrases like 'God uses' children, because I think the matter of God's commission is much more subtle than that and I hope to show that in the matter of commission, children and young people bring their own gifts or 'flavour' to what they undertake. Further, children can be called especially to disturb the adult order of things where people think they are in control and can do what they like. This disturbance is at the heart of creating a new space in which God's message or justice can be seen to take root through children.

The commission to become fully human: Adam and Eve

I want to return to the Garden of Eden, and the first human beings. Most paintings of Adam and Eve show the couple as adults, but I am going to suggest that the creation stories which are related in the first two chapters of Genesis offer us insights into the way God finds *children* worthy of commissioning.

Adam and the woman are offered to us as new humans and the first of God's children, but the Garden of Eden itself is also significant as the space in which God's children are located:

And the Lord God planted a garden in Eden, to the east, and He placed there the human He had fashioned. And the Lord God caused

to sprout from the soil every tree lovely to look at and good for food,
and the tree of life was in the midst of the garden, and the tree of
knowledge, good and evil.   (Genesis 2.8–9)[1]

The Garden of Eden is a special, particular and enclosed space, a world
within a world, within which the human beings can be nurtured. In
this sense, the Garden of Eden is a womb-like space in which Adam
is perfectly safe, perfectly cared-for and in communion with the
Creator. Yet Adam is not a merely passive recipient of nourishment
and divine love; he is commissioned to interact with his environment,
to 'till it and watch it' and to eat its fruits. This is not the arduous
toil that exists outside the Garden, for it is continually watered and
the ground is fertile. Adam is offered the opportunity to delight in
the garden, to play in it, and to discover its loveliness.

Further:

And the Lord God fashioned from the soil each beast of the field and
each fowl of the heavens and brought each to the human to see what
he would call it, and whatever the human called a living creature,
that was its name.   (Genesis 2.19)[2]

Again, this is like a serious game. God brings new creatures to Adam
and Adam names them. God does not say 'that's a silly name' or say
that its 'real' name is such and such, but accepts the human's descrip-
tion of the world which he inhabits. Adam is commissioned to get
his own hands dirty in the soil of his world, to eat its fruit and to
know and name everything around him. As God has delighted and
played in the process of creation, so the humans in the Garden of
Eden are invited to play with the created world. This playfulness is
even echoed in the Hebrew text with punning or echoic words.[3] We
saw earlier that the idea of delight and play being embedded in
the unfolding of creation is also echoed in Proverbs 8.30–31, where
Wisdom is imagined playing in the world and delighting in it.

If we read the creation stories as a way in which we are shown
how divine interaction between God and God's children works, then
we learn a number of interesting things. First, God not only calls

---

[1] Robert Alter, *The Five Books of Moses* (New York: W. W. Norton, 2004), p. 21.
[2] Alter, *The Five Books of Moses*, p. 23.
[3] 'adam/'adamah; 'arum/'arumim.

each of us into being, but commissions us to find out about our world, engaging with it through the senses. It cannot be incidental that we are told that the trees are lovely to look at, or that the new humans are to eat the fruit, or that the animals are brought to Adam. The proto-humans are naked in the garden, their skin exposed to the touch and experience of the natural world. We repeat these experiences with our children every time we point out a field of poppies, buy them ice creams at the seaside, visit a farm where they can meet the animals, or let them jump naked into a paddling pool on a hot day. These 'treats' recall the first experiences of the first humans in Genesis and they give us an indication of what God commissions from children in the business of growing and becoming: delight, pleasure, play, and exploration of the world around them.

Hans Urs Von Balthasar writes:

> But, for the person who is open to the absolute, there exists another kind of amazement with regard to nature as we know it outside our-selves. To be sure, the seed shoots up, spring returns again, and we take note of all the varieties of animals. But is it not amazing that all of this *is*? Is not the splendor of a flower or the imploring or grateful look of a dog just as amazing as the functioning of a new airplane . . . ? 'The Father is greater than I' lies hidden in all human experiences. God remains, even in what he, the ever greater one, has handed over to his creatures as their own.[4]

Balthasar suggests that we should seek to hold on to the child's capacity for amazement, for awe and wonder at the creation. We can say that this connects us to primordial experiences as laid out in the creation stories in Genesis and thereby also to the profound commis-sion from God 'hidden in all human experiences'. The first commission which God gives each one of us is to become human.

On this reading, the story of the Fall takes on another cast. In chapter 2, God tells Adam

> From every fruit of the garden you may surely eat. But from the tree of knowledge, good and evil, you shall not eat, for on the day you eat from it, you are doomed to die.   (Genesis 2.16–17)[5]

---

[4] H. Balthasar, *Unless You Become Like This Child* (San Francisco: Ignatius Press, 1991), p. 47.
[5] Alter, *The Five Books of Moses*, p. 21.

In chapter 3, however,

> The woman saw that the tree was good for eating and that it was
> lust to the eyes and the tree was lovely to look at, and she took of its
> fruit and ate, and she also gave to her man, and he ate. And the eyes
> of the two were opened. (Genesis 3.6–7)[6]

What is happening here? Theologically, this is a crucial and irrevoc-
able moment, when 'man's first disobedience and the fruit of the
forbidden tree' cuts us off from God until Jesus, God's own Son,
redeems us. Yet, if we return to the idea of Adam and Eve as children
commissioned by the Creator to become fully human, what *else* can
we understand to be going on?

The tree delights the eye – more than that, in Alter's translation it is
'lust to the eyes', tremendously desirable. It is definitely good to eat.
If we think of Eve as a child exploring the world, then we can imagine
her poised between two experiences. She has been exploring with her
body, delighting in what she sees, savouring what she tastes, touching
and smelling the earth and the food, just as any child does. It makes
sense to her to respond to what her senses tell her. On the other hand,
her parent has given her a strict prohibition on this lovely thing. We
need to explore both the temptation and the prohibition.

Work done on delayed gratification in the 1960s and 1970s by the
psychologist Walter Mischel and collectively known as the Stanford
'marshmallow' test gives us a way to think about the temptation, if
we posit that Adam and Eve are rendered to us essentially as children
exploring their new world. The test was extremely simple. Young
children (aged 4–6 years) were left alone for 15 minutes in an empty
room with a marshmallow (or similar) on a plate and told they could
either eat it straight away or, if they put off eating it until the researcher
came back, they would be given another one, so they would have
two. A few children ate the marshmallow straight away. Of those
that did not, a significant number sniffed at, handled, or touched
their tongues to the marshmallow, sensing it.[7] Some dealt with the
temptation by distracting themselves, trying not to think about the

---

[6] Alter, *The Five Books of Moses*, pp. 24–5.

[7] At the time of writing a version of this test has been made into an advertisement for Haribo
sweets in which none of the children offered a Haribo can resist eating them no matter how
hard they try to hold out for another one, with the conclusion 'Haribos are just too good'.

marshmallow. Many children eventually gave in. It is perhaps even more interesting that the researcher later discovered a correlation between the ability for self-control and success in later life.[8] The serpent holds out the first part of the offer – have it now; God promises a better future as long as they resist. Adam and Eve try to resist the temptation but they cannot last out for ever. In the end they submit to the desire of their bodily senses over what might lie in the future. They discover something about being human.

In addition, what the serpent also does is to tip Eve into another critical phase of being human: taking risks. Adam and Eve have been fairly warned, but they have no idea what 'doomed to die' means – until they find out.

I remember as a small child the first time I was stung by a bee. I was sitting inside a bush covered in flowers looking at the butterflies landing on them, and trying to touch them. As a bee buzzed in and settled on a flower, I was taken with its furry back and lovely colours and grabbed it. Unsurprisingly it stung me. I couldn't believe how painful it was as I ran screaming from the bush for my mother. The pain, however, was not as great as the shock, the idea that beautiful nature contained such deadly things that could hurt you. My mother, examining my throbbing hand, said, 'I told you not to touch the bees.'

For God's children, testing the boundaries, risk, and disobedience bring a new element to being human. Now they know that they are vulnerable. They know that they are naked, not just in the sexual sense, but in the sense of the fragility of bodies; the fact that we can be hurt and that we will die. The tree is the knowledge of good and evil: the goodness and beauty of the world, but also its pain and suffering where you can't have your cake and eat it. This is what God knows about the way the created world evolves and now they know it too. They are not immortal. Their bodies will fail and they will die.

So the Fall can be seen as a very serious lesson in the experience of growing up. Our children experience it every time they fall off

---

[8] W. Mischel, 'Processes in Delay of Gratification', in L. Berkowitz (ed.), *Advances in Experimental Social Psychology* (San Diego, CA: Academic Press, 1974), vol. 7, pp. 249–92. W. Mischel, Y. Shoda and M. L. Rodriguez, 'Delay of Gratification in Children', *Science* 244 (1989), pp. 933–8.

their bikes, break their arm jumping out of a tree, burn themselves on the irresistibly beautiful flame, or eat something delicious that makes them sick. Theology has ramped this up to ontological and existential arguments about our ultimate destiny, and we cannot pretend this depth to the narratives does not exist, but it seems to me that one of the reasons this narrative feels so powerful to us is precisely because it is familiar not just to our minds or our spiritual lives but to our *bodies*. We have all eaten the forbidden fruit and been sorry afterwards; yet we live in a fallen world and that is how we grow and learn.

We all know what happens next. Adam and the woman are expelled from the Garden. In one sense this is like a birth experience, the humans are ejected from a warm safe environment where they are perfectly nourished and cared for into a hostile and harsh world where they must learn to fend for themselves. They cannot go back to the source of life. The commission to be fully human continues. God tells them the harsh truth about the facts of human life, about work, childbearing and death. It is important that God does not just kick Adam and the woman out and leave them to it; in this new phase of their existence, he clothes them, protecting their vulnerable skin from the elements. The parent creator continues to care for the children, but now God is guiding, not holding their hands. God's children have learned the hard way through play and experiment and risk; now they are equipped to carry out God's will for them in the world. Though they no longer live in Eden, and have to struggle in a world of violence and pain, through them and through other human beings, God's love and care for the children will become known again and the way back to God understood. Adam's first act of naming on the other side of the Garden is to name the woman. She is now Eve.[9]

The problem with adults

So if we reframe the creation stories in Genesis to see Adam and Eve as children of God, then we can see that God calls each of us

---

[9] Alter points out that her name sounds like the Aramaic word for serpent – as if she takes with her a memory of the point of departure, or even of the origin of life as we experience it.

into being and commissions us with the task of being human. That commission begins before birth and follows us into the way we as children explore and discover the world. But one of the reasons why God finds children worthy of commission is because something happens to adults which makes it harder and harder to hold on to what God asks of us. Perhaps the Eden story offers some reasons why it is so: it is difficult to make one's way in the world, to conceive, bear and raise healthy children. The business of working and providing is right and proper, but if we lose the delight, the play and the joy in the world God has given; if we forget to love and tend the creation, then we start to fall prey to a spiritual amnesia that leads us to replace God's charitable and relational promptings in us with our own certainties and desires. Other stories in the book of Genesis, such as the murder of Abel and the wickedness in Sodom, leave us in no doubt that we are in an adult world of violence and disobedience to God far from the Garden. We learn very quickly that adults are good at forgetting about God except when they want to control God for themselves.

So in other places where we see God actively commissioning children in Scripture, it can jolt adults out of their complacency, or enable them to hear a hard message about God's ways with the world, or face them with their own amnesia. We are probably all familiar with the way we can be caught out when children mention things to others we would much rather they hadn't said, but beyond our embarrassment, we might like to reflect on the keenness of their observation of the adult world and their way of cutting through the endless dressings and coatings we put on our relationships and ways of expressing things.

The commission to speak God's difficult word

Then I said 'Ah, Lord God! Truly I do not know how to
    speak, for I am only a boy.' But the LORD said to me,
'Do not say "I am only a boy";
for you shall go to all to whom I send you,
and you shall speak whatever I command you.
Do not be afraid of them,
for I am with you to deliver you, says the LORD.'

Then the LORD put out his hand and touched my mouth;
  and the LORD said to me,
'Now I have put my words in your mouth.
See, today I appoint you over nations and over kingdoms,
To pluck up and to pull down,
To destroy and to overthrow,
To build and to plant.'

(Jeremiah 1.6–10)

The commissioning of Jeremiah as a prophet of God, commissioned to speak difficult and demanding words to the people, carries with it some important elements. We cannot say how young Jeremiah is; his protest that he is only a 'boy' might just mean that he is relatively young to have any real authority and is inexperienced in communicating.[10] But given the movement from God's calling him to be as an unborn child, it is not unreasonable to imagine a young person who still has what St Jerome calls 'the grace of boyhood'.[11] The 'stylized features'[12] of the call narrative should not prevent us from asking what this commission means in terms of how children and young people respond to the call they recognize in themselves. God's response is to say that it doesn't matter about Jeremiah's inexperience or lack of authority, because commission, as in the case of Adam and Eve, does not mean being thrown out into the world and left to get on with it. God goes with those who go forward in their commission and supports them as they struggle with the task to which they are called. They can be confident that this means something real, and that they have genuine gifts which have important and long-lasting effects. The call narrative offers a partnership between the prophetic vocation and God, in which the person is helped and empowered by God as his gifts develop. But more to the point, this young, insignificant person is promised that his speech makes a difference. All we are asked to do is to say 'yes!' of our own volition in response to the commission.

---

[10] See, for example, Allen's translation of this section in L. Allen, *Jeremiah: A Commentary* (Louisville, KY: John Knox Press, 2008), p. 23; W. McKane, *The International Critical Commentary, Jeremiah: Volume 1: 1–25* (Edinburgh: T&T Clark, 1986), pp. 7–8.

[11] Jerome, *Commentary on Jeremiah* (trans. Michael Graves; Ancient Christian Texts; Downers Grove, IL: Inter-Varsity Press, 2012), p. 3.

[12] W. Brueggemann, *A Commentary on Jeremiah: Exile and Homecoming* (Grand Rapids, MI: Eerdmans, 1998), p. 24.

A social worker once told me that she had met a child who, when asked her name, replied 'Shut up Samantha!' Every time she spoke, this had been flung back at her, so she assumed that that was what she was called. That's an extreme example, but it's common for all of us to seek to silence our children when they ask annoying questions, chatter on happily through things we're trying to concentrate on or simply ask 'Why?' fifty thousand times a day. Worse, adults sometimes just tune children out, so that their communications are met with indulgence, silence or indifference. Jeremiah's story tells us different. There is a God-language in the young which will cut through all adult attempts to silence it. No matter how much we use our adult power and superior vocabulary, the commission of God *cannot* be stopped. And when we do hear them, it might not be a language to our liking.

We saw in Chapter 1 how God calls the boy Samuel, but the commission entrusted to Samuel is both surprising and serious:

> Then the LORD said to Samuel, 'See, I am about to do something in Israel that will make both ears of anyone who hears of it tingle. On that day I will fulfil against Eli all that I have spoken concerning his house, from beginning to end. For I have told him that I am about to punish his house for ever, for the iniquity that he knew, because his sons were blaspheming God, and he did not restrain them. Therefore I swear to the house of Eli that the iniquity of Eli's house shall not be expiated by sacrifice or offering for ever.'
>
> (1 Samuel 3.11–14)

The back story to all this is contained in 1 Samuel 2.27–36. Although some of the pieces of this text are disputed and unclear, the writer of this narrative has set out the curse that has been placed on Eli and his family. Clearly, however, Eli's priestly ministry has fallen short and he thinks he can keep God's wrath away by his Temple service and by doing what he wants. Apparently unabashed by the testimony of the man of God, Eli now has to face the word of God delivered through the mouth of a child. This is not an easy message, but one to make your 'ears tingle'.

But there is more to this narrative than just the message. Eli has forgotten what it really means to serve God. His job is to oversee the sacrifices to God and to see that the worship is properly observed but he has been giving the sacrificial meat to his family, stealing from those who have brought donations to God's altar and cheating both them and God. Who is most likely to see this happening if not his protégé Samuel? The child stands in the middle of this behaviour and surely knows what is going on and is perhaps expected to turn a blind eye to it or to be complicit in it in some way. Yet Eli discovers that Samuel is not 'just' a child, but one who speaks God's truth. It is ironic that it is his master Eli who points the way for Samuel to respond to God's call, because it is God's word that comes straight back to him with its powerful condemnation of corruption in the very place which is supposed to be holy.

So if we bring our children to baptism and profess that we will bring them up as Christians, we should be very clear that we know what burden that places on us to be parents and godparents bringing up children in faith. Otherwise if we fall short, then we should not be surprised that our children both notice and name it. I will call this the 'Samuel effect'.

In fact I saw this quite recently in a church where it pays not to ignore the presence of children. A young mother (not a churchgoer) came into the church to attend a wedding. When the wedding was over and she was getting ready to leave, one of her two young children asked about the room at the side called the 'Reconciliation Room'. She asked what it said and what it meant, but the mother didn't know. One of the older church members, who had been sitting in front of them, explained that it was a place you could go to talk to the priest about your life. You could tell him about things you had done wrong or that were worrying you. And it was very important to tell the truth.

'Are you going in there now?' the younger child asked the church lady.

'No,' she replied.

'Well you should, because you told a lie.'

Uncomfortable laughter. 'No I didn't.'

'Yes you did. You said to [the bride's mother] "You look lovely". And then straight afterwards you said to [a friend] that she was too fat for that dress.'

And the older child helpfully held the door open for her.

The Samuel effect will definitely make your ears tingle . . .

God's commission for children can
be announced through others

In Scripture, in the case of the just born, God's commission to children can be announced to others by angels or prophets or priests. One of the important aspects of this is that the announcement creates a shape for the child's life, which others are required to think about and to be prepared for. So, Isaac's and Ishmael's births come with future promise of great nations. God promises to establish his covenant with Isaac. Hannah's child is commissioned to the Lord's service, as is Samson, commissioned from birth to be a deliverer from the Philistines.

Perhaps, though, the most important commission from birth is given to us through the annunciation and birth of Jesus. In the parallel stories of the annunciations to Mary and Zechariah, the angel makes it clear that these children must be nurtured for their specific commissions from God. The as yet unborn John 'must never drink wine or strong drink; even before his birth he will be filled with the Holy Spirit' (Luke 1.15). It matters that parents are prepared for the point at which the children will accept their commission and say 'yes!', otherwise they will not be able to offer the necessary support and care for the children's spiritual growth and reflection. And for parents this is not necessarily an easy task. Allowing children to explore their God-given talents and special calling can mean sacrifice and struggle.

Watching the Olympics in 2012, I was struck by the remarkable back stories of some of the athletes. Parents, aunts, uncles, cousins, brothers and sisters, coaches and mentors often gave up vast swathes of their lives to help the athletes go through their exhaustive gruelling training, getting up at 4 a.m. to drive their children to swimming pools or meets, looking after them and encouraging them when injury or setbacks happened. They cried with them and consoled them when things went badly and the athletes felt like giving up, celebrated when things went well, but in general sacrificed money for equipment, time for training, because their children knew they had a gift they had to pursue. Thinking about these people, the ones who didn't get the medal or to stand on the podium, made me think more about what it would have been like to nurture children whose spiritual destiny in the world of the Bible was so huge. I have not been the only person to wonder about this.

Mary and Jesus as children: Apocryphal infancy gospels[13]

One of the things which is tantalizingly missing from the canonical books of the Bible is detail about the background of the Holy Family. We are told astonishing things about the Annunciation to Mary, that a virgin will conceive a son and that her child will be God's own Son and that through him, human beings will be saved. This commission is so huge, it is a wonder we don't hold our breath waiting for Mary's reply, 'let it be with me according to your word' (Luke 1.38). Yet there are all kinds of questions we might immediately want to ask about all this. Why was Mary chosen? What was it like to be pregnant with such a child? What was it like to bring him up? How exactly was a little child like Jesus expected to answer his commission or to realize his human and divine status as the Son of God?

It is not surprising then that there are a number of 'infancy gospels' which give us some of the missing information. These gospels draw heavily on the accounts of God's commission to others in the canonical Scriptures, but in other places they are fanciful wonder stories and suppliers of detail for theological ideas such as the virgin birth. But there is also a deeper motif, I think, which is to try and understand more of God's commission to human beings, even if they sometimes seem to be going over the top in imagining it. It is worth taking a look.

The Protoevangelium of James (also the gospel of Pseudo-Matthew which amplifies it) fills in detail about Jesus' grandparents, the childhood of Mary and segues into the Annunciation and birth of Jesus. Jesus' grandparents are Anna and Joachim and, like other important women in Scripture, Anna is childless. In Pseudo-Matthew, Joachim is a herder of sheep and a righteous man who gives his wealth to widows and orphans, but despite being married to Anna for 20 years, they have no child. Joachim feels disgraced by this and Anna is in

---

[13] These are collected in J. Elliott (ed.), *The Apocryphal New Testament: A Collection of Apocryphal Christian Literature in an English Translation based on M R James* (Oxford: Oxford University Press, 2005 [1995]). Also see B. Ehrman and Z. Plese, *The Apocryphal Gospels: Texts and Translation* (Oxford: Oxford University Press, 2011).

despair, mocked by the fertility of the natural world around her. Joachim is told to put off his disgrace by an angel saying that Anna will have a daughter, and he is to offer a burnt offering in gratitude. Anna gives birth to Mary and to give thanks they decide to dedicate her in service to God, and at the age of three, precociously developed both in physical robustness and spiritual awareness, she is sent to live in the Temple. The texts make much of the fact that Mary leaves her parents for temple service without so much as looking back, dancing for joy on the steps of the Temple. She has responded with joy to her vocation and is God's child now. But when Mary is 12, the priests can't keep her because her menstruation will defile the Temple, so they organize a lottery to choose who is going to look after her. Joseph gets her, but he is less than pleased, because he is old and already has children. Yet he cannot reject her so he takes her as his ward. He takes her into his household and goes away. The Annunciation happens and Mary becomes pregnant and she hides out at Elizabeth's house. When Joseph returns she is six months pregnant, so he is less than pleased with this so-called holy virgin of the Temple. Joseph doesn't believe that she hasn't had sex and threatens to throw her out, but is told by an angel that her story is true. The priests do not believe either Joseph or Mary. The story then passes on into the nativity in which Mary gives birth in a cave and a woman called Salome, who also does not believe Mary is physically a virgin, examines her to find out – and gets her fingers burned (literally).

This story fills in the blanks about Jesus' parents and grandparents and describes the religious and devoted context in which he is conceived and born. The text also tries to get at what it must have been like for the young Mary. She is clearly a special child, an only child. Her life is dedicated to God and her mind is bent on serving God, but she is also physically healthy and strong; she has to be spiritual but also physically able to conceive, bear and bring up a healthy child. She is brought up to this important purpose. The writer(s) of the text try to imagine what kind of child and what kind of upbringing would bring about a depth of spirituality and devotion to accept the commission from God to bear Jesus. What gave her that spiritual depth, or the trust to allow her body to carry a child, when the result would be shame and disgrace? The writer(s) are also aware of the sheer incomprehensibility of the virgin birth and through the dissenters and doubters in the story there is wrestling back and forth between those who point to the commonsense explanation for a pregnancy – sex – and the miraculous workings of God for a deeper, higher purpose. When Salome gets her fingers burned, the question is left with the reader – do *you* now believe it? Do you now believe that God calls and commissions children and young people through their spiritual awareness and growth in this way, even to processes and events which are impossible? If you don't and, like Doubting Thomas later on, want the bodily proof of God's action in the world, maybe you risk burning your fingers.

The apocryphal gospels offer us Mary as a child, but there is also the question of what on earth Jesus was like a child. In the canonical Scriptures he is a baby wrapped in swaddling clothes and laid in a manger, the receiver of worship and gifts, under threat from Herod. But we know little else about how he survives and is brought up. The infancy gospel of Thomas[14] fills in these gaps too.

This text gives us fanciful stories about a little boy with extraordinary powers who has to work out what to do with them. He is a little bit like the children and young people in the TV series *Heroes* or one of young people of the X-Men, extraordinarily gifted in a world which is frightened of people with gifts. The Christmas carol image of 'gentle Jesus meek and mild' is not to be found here. If in the world of the carols it feels cloyingly unrealistic when children are exhorted to be 'mild, obedient, good as he', we would not want our children to be like *this* Jesus. He is neither gentle nor quiet nor good. Jesus is not so devoted as Mary; in fact he is, as Terry Jones might say, a very naughty boy. Aged five, Jesus makes clay sparrows on the Sabbath (which is not allowed, because it is work and contravenes the commandment to keep the Sabbath as a rest day and holy) and he turns them into living birds which fly away when Joseph comes to tell him off; Jesus curses and kills other children who mess up his game or bump into him with his divine but undirected power, but resurrects a dead child to exonerate himself when the child died

---

[14] This infancy gospel can also be found online at <www.gnosis.org/library/inftoma.htm>. The writer Philip Pullman used this text as the basis for his novel *The Good Man Jesus and the Scoundrel Christ* (London: Viking, 2010).

in an accident and people want to blame Jesus. Mary and Joseph are beside themselves. Joseph has to go around hushing things up and is sick with worry about the various attempts to get Jesus to behave in school. But Jesus does help his father by miraculously fixing his carpentry problems and healing things like snake bites, which I suppose is handy. The text then segues into the story of Jesus being left behind in the Temple. He has left his uncontrolled and destructive behaviour behind. He has mastered his emotions and now understands more about his remarkable gifts.

The writer of the text is clearly trying to understand through imagination what it must have been like for the child Jesus. There is perhaps a Harry Potter-ish feel to the narrative, when strange, even destructive things happen which are not explained until Jesus receives teaching and a way of understanding what it all means. Yet the writer weaves naturalistic elements into all the miraculous events, so that we can feel that this is a real child that is being described. Jesus plays in the street with the other children, climbs about in people's houses, follows his big brother around, watches his father at work and tells the mother of the resurrected child to give him some milk.

While this doesn't help us understand more about God's commission, it does raise questions about how children, dependent on their parents, are given the time and space they need to understand their gifts and their place in God's economy. How on earth did Jesus get to the point where he came to John for baptism? What experiences in his childhood, what experience of Temple worship and the life of prayer and devotion prepared him for the public announcement of his ministry?

Also, how far was Jesus' 'yes!' to God, if we imagine that moment being bound up with the event in which Jesus is left behind in Jerusalem, something which conditioned his later actions in relation to the Temple? If it was difficult for Jesus' parents to know exactly what Jesus needed to explore and respond to his vocation, how far do those powerful recognitions of God's reality forge difficult clashes in later life? If we see Jesus as an older child telling Mary and Joseph that he must be in his Father's house, then perhaps this foreshadows Jesus' outbreak of violent fury about the traders in the Temple. There was nothing odd about the traders in the

Temple – their presence was accepted practice – yet Jesus' commission brings outrage and upset. The traders' ears must have been tingling *that* day. We will look in Chapter 5 at the possible effects on Jesus' family of his profound and obedient acceptance of God's desire for his life.

God's commission emerges from context

In the film *Home Alone*, a little child has to defend his family from determined but bungling burglars. Kevin is just a kid and so the burglars assume he can easily be intimidated or overcome. But Kevin has an advantage: he knows his home much better than they do. He uses his toys, a video, some firecrackers, his brother's pet spider and the home's Christmas decorations to foil the burglars and keep them away from his territory and his family. It's a David and Goliath scenario.

> When the words that David spoke were heard, they repeated them before Saul; and he sent for him. David said to Saul, 'Let no one's heart fail because of him; your servant will go and fight with this Philistine.' Saul said to David, 'You are not able to go against this Philistine to fight with him; for you are just a boy, and he has been a warrior from his youth.' But David said to Saul, 'Your servant used to keep sheep for his father; and whenever a lion or a bear came, and took a lamb from the flock, I went after it and struck it down, rescuing the lamb from its mouth; and if it turned against me, I would catch it by the jaw, strike it down, and kill it. Your servant has killed both lions and bears; and this uncircumcised Philistine shall be like one of them, since he has defied the armies of the living God.' David said, 'The LORD, who saved me from the paw of the lion and from the paw of the bear, will save me from the hand of this Philistine.' So Saul said to David, 'Go, and may the LORD be with you!'
> Saul clothed David with his armour; he put a bronze helmet on his head and clothed him with a coat of mail. David strapped Saul's sword over the armour, and he tried in vain to walk, for he was not used to them. Then David said to Saul, 'I cannot walk with these; for I am not used to them.' So David removed them. Then he took his staff in his hand, and chose five smooth stones from the wadi, and put them in his shepherd's bag, in the pouch; his sling was in his hand, and he drew near to the Philistine.   (1 Samuel 17.31–40)

The point about David is that the gifts he has to defeat Goliath come from his life as a child, not from the lives and procedures of adults. David can't be a champion wearing armour and waving a sword. But David is prepared to accept the commission, because he has gifts honed from his early experiences. He knows how to throw the stones at animals which would hurt the sheep. He knows which stones work best and he is not afraid of large or fierce enemies. As far as he is concerned he already has everything he needs, including the conviction that God is with him and will help him overcome the threat, just as he has experienced in his life as a shepherd boy.

This tells us something important about the way God finds children worthy of commission. God does not expect children to do more than they are capable of, nor do children have to conform to adult roles before they are ready. Again we find the issue at hand being reframed. For the adult Saul Goliath is a warrior enemy. No one can fight him except on his own terms, covered in armour and meeting him with adult weapons. But David treats Goliath as another lion or bear who is threatening the sheep. This is where he feels comfortable and this is where his spirituality has been honed. Goliath is simply not prepared for the child's reframing of the situation, nor for the prospect of the smooth stones from the wadi which can have such devastating effect.

Children then can completely blindside us and knock us off our feet. Too often, this is difficult for adults to cope with and we struggle to get the upper hand, perhaps by seeking to impose our rules, make the children fall under the weight of the armour or the sword and refuse to let them bring their experience, understanding and wisdom to bear, lest we be made to look small. It's a common feature of our society that we try to remake children in our own image, and we note that, increasingly, children react to this by inheriting our adult neuroses, about risk, about body image and weight, about clothes and material possessions. Children are constantly being urged to grow up, rather than just grow. Yet the story of David and Goliath shows that if children are given the space and time to explore their gifts, then the commission to grow and flourish gives them the tools to prosper in ways we have trouble imagining. Somehow we have to trust children to be children.

Commission emerges from complexity: the little servant girl

Another important illustration of how children contribute to the commission of God to bring about God's purposes is shown in stories of greater complexity, in which a child is a vital part of events which allow God to be glorified:

> Naaman, commander of the army of the king of Aram, was a great man and in high favour with his master, because by him the LORD had given victory to Aram. The man, though a mighty warrior, suffered from leprosy. Now the Arameans on one of their raids had taken a young girl captive from the land of Israel, and she served Naaman's wife. She said to her mistress, 'If only my lord were with the prophet who is in Samaria! He would cure him of his leprosy.' So Naaman went in and told his lord just what the girl from the land of Israel had said. And the king of Aram said, 'Go then, and I will send along a letter to the king of Israel.'   (2 Kings 5.1–5)

The child at the heart of this narrative is a little servant girl. She is a captive and has no status and no agency. She can have no direct effect on the central issue, which is Naaman's leprosy, but her voice enters into the consciousness of her mistress and through her reaches Naaman and the king of Aram himself. It is interesting that this voice, which transmits a message of God's power and healing grace from the bottom upwards, passes all the way from a female slave-child to the actions of kings. The little girl acts as a prophet, prophesying a future in which healing is possible and speaking God-language into the situation. The child, identifying a space in which that God-language can be heard, utters it, and God's word does not ever come back empty. It is through that little child's word that Naaman comes to be healed and God to be glorified. Was it perhaps that response to God in a little child that prompted Jesus to name Naaman as the route through which God was glorified in Luke 4.27?

The story of the little servant girl suggests that we should not think that children have no agency; instead we should understand that through their speech and actions, new things can come about in the lives of adults. For example, I was once visiting a person in a hospice who was dying. The person did not want to talk about the fact that she was dying and was studiously pretending that she was going to get better and go home. All the other adults were colluding with this and generally humouring her, even though everyone knew that she would not be going home again. I took my children to visit her and as we were sitting outside, one of my sons suddenly piped up, 'Are you going to stay here until you die?' There was a stunned, uncomfortable and then deeply embarrassed silence before everyone started talking at once about anything else they could think of. Later, I got a telephone call asking me not to bring my children again as 'she can't cope with it'. But when I visited again, the nurses told me that the person had begun to accept that she would not get better and they had been able to discuss some important things with her about her will and her funeral. The building of that bridge to acceptance had started on the day my son asked her if she would remain until she died.

Commission as an effect in the life of God's people

Before we leave the matter of how children become aware of God's call to them to flourish and grow and how they respond with a positive 'yes!' to that commission to be God-language in the world, it might be helpful to look at how commission and children also work as metaphor in the Bible. The 'children' part of the phrase can denote the importance of genealogical descent for the Israelites, the sense of belonging to a community by being born and raised within it. In this sense, the fact of being called by God to be a person of this lineage, history and faith is deeply embedded in the psyche of the community. We can see how this sense of being a child of the Israelite community and a child of God is part of any new child's spiritual formation. In Exodus 13.1 we see God impressing on Moses that God does not want any child to die; rather that the children of Israel must know for ever the power and passion of the divine intention to save. God tells Moses, 'Consecrate unto Me each firstborn, breach of each womb among the Israelites in man and in beast – it is Mine'.[15] Firstborn children, bursting upon the world, can become God's priests, linking the community to the living God, while the firstborn animals are to be sacrificed. A few verses further on, God makes it clear that Israel's children are to be steeped in salvation history, so that the Passover will become the most powerful memory

---

[15] Alter, *The Five Books of Moses*, p. 385.

made present of God's desire to save his people: 'And you shall tell your son on that day, saying, "For the sake of what the Lord did for me when I went out of Egypt".'[16] The Passover, then, in which the blood of the Passover lamb sprinkled on the door entrances causes death to pass by, becomes not only the event by which God's desire to save children is demonstrated, but confirms in each Jewish child each time Passover is celebrated that she is one whom God has saved, and with whom the divine relationship is to be acknowledged with joy, a repeated 'yes!' to God's call.[17] Jesus was also one of those children in whom the miracle of Passover and its meaning was instilled, asking the question 'why is this night different from all other nights?' It is perhaps significant that it is after the Passover festivities that we find him as a boy staying behind in Jerusalem soaking up the meaning of the Scriptures, and that we find him celebrating the Passover and identifying with its themes of sacrifice and salvation immediately before his arrest, trial and death. On both occasions we find him accepting God's commission and seeking to know and follow God's will for his life and for the world.

It is important that when Israelite children are commissioned by God to serve their community they are properly nurtured and encouraged. The prophet Amos utters a warning:

> And I raised up some of your
> children to be prophets
> and some of your youths to be nazirites.
> Is it not indeed so, O people of Israel?[18]
> says the LORD.
> But you made the nazirites
> drink wine
> and commanded the prophets,
> saying, 'You shall not prophesy,'

---

[16] Alter, *The Five Books of Moses*, p. 385; cf. Exodus 12.26–27.

[17] Of course, the story in Exodus 11 shows a death-dealing God who strikes down the firstborn of the Egyptians even as the Israelites are spared. Does this not undermine the argument that God does not want any child to die? We can understand this by seeing that access to God's salvation depends on having a real and productive relationship. Pharaoh's behaviour towards the Israelites cuts his people off from God's compassion and mercy and he is left adrift in a world plagued by natural disaster and death. It is not perhaps surprising then that in Exodus 12.32 Pharaoh essentially asks Moses to pray for him.

[18] Translated 'children of Israel' in the King James Version.

So, I will press you down in your place,
just as a cart presses down
when it is full of sheaves.

(Amos 2.11–13)

The calling and commissioning of children and young people is to be
properly fostered by the community and getting in the way of such
spiritual growth and formation is not what God wants.

Just as each child born into the Israelite community was tied
into its spiritual formation by ritual and culture, so 'the children of
Israel' becomes a metaphor tied to the commissioning of the nation
by God to be a distinctive cultic presence. The children of Israel have
to learn what their commission to be and to grow as God's holy
nation really is. Just as children can be agents of God-language, so
the call to Israel to be ethically holy, a light to the nations, emerges
as a vocation into which the nation must grow. The Israelite community is constantly called to say 'yes!' to God in faithfulness, yet like
a child making mistakes, learning and growing, so Israel falters and
has to learn. In Isaiah 48, for example, God announces his presence
as 'the LORD your God, who teaches you for your own good, who
leads you in the way you should go' (v. 17). Israel turned aside from
this parental guidance, cutting off the children who would have
multiplied fruitfully under God, 'your offspring would have been
like the sand' (v. 19). Yet here is a new beginning for the wayward
children: 'I will give you as a light to the nations, that my salvation
may reach to the end of the earth' (Isaiah 49.6). God now promises
that the divine love is more constant even than a human loving
parent: 'Can a woman forget her nursing-child, or show no compassion for the child of her womb? Even these may forget, yet I will not
forget you' (Isaiah 49.15). The children of Israel as a faith community
may fall away from God, but, says the prophet, the constancy of
God as a living parent and guide is assured: the vocation to be a
holy nation and the commission to be an example to others is never
withdrawn. It is up to Israel to respond, to continue to say 'yes!' to
God. When Jesus assumes his public ministry, this is a message that
he will repeat. His own people, in whose community he has been
brought up, have pursued self-interest and forgotten to put their
commission from God first. I hear echoes of both Amos and Isaiah

in the 'Woe to' passages of Matthew 23, and perhaps especially when Jesus says, 'Jerusalem, Jerusalem, the city that kills the prophets and stones those who are sent to it! How often have I desired to gather your children together as a hen gathers her brood under her wings, and you were not willing!' (Matthew 23.37). In the time of Jesus, those who say 'yes!' to God and are faithful to God's call and commission are still being rejected, yet the love and longing of God for the people still remains. I find these words of grief, anger and desire, helpful in further elucidating the Jesus of Matthew 18.6 who threatens those who might cause a child to falter.

The commission to build a kingdom fit for children

In the prophecy surrounding the birth of John the Baptist, Zechariah is told about the effect his son will have in preparing people for the in-breaking of God's kingdom:

> He will turn many of the people of Israel to the Lord their God. With the spirit and power of Elijah he will go before him, to turn the hearts of parents to their children, and the disobedient to the wisdom of the righteous, to make ready a people prepared for the Lord.
>
> (Luke 1.16–17)

The Gospels begin to hint that the kingdom of God breaking into the lives of people now must start from the bottom up. The least respected and thought of have significance in God's economy; the ones who come last are the most desired and will be offered an equal share. The metaphor of the last becoming the first works for age as well as status, and we will see later how this matters in thinking about what a Christian community might look like.

Jesus startles his own community when he calls a child and puts the child among the disciples who are arguing about who is the greatest in the kingdom. Jesus says:

> Whoever becomes humble like this child is the greatest in the kingdom of heaven. Whoever welcomes one such child in my name welcomes me.
>
> (Matthew 18.4–5)

It is important to remember that despite the importance of having children in an age when so few would make it to adulthood, socially and culturally, children as persons were at the bottom of the heap. In Jesus' time a quarter of children would die in their first year; half of all children would die before they were ten.[19] Reidar Aasgaard tells us that this meant that the relationship between the head of the household and the children was complex, since the household needed children to continue the family line, but at the same time the lives of children were precarious and all the power was concentrated in the adult males.[20] In general, however, to be a child was to be vulnerable, powerless, and at risk. In public life, the child had no existence as a separate individual, only as an extension of a household. Yet Jesus turns the whole social order on its head. God's kingdom belongs to one who is, or is like, a child. This is not a theoretical teaching point; Jesus takes a child and makes everyone recognize who he or she is. The disciples have to look, acknowledge, respect someone who has no status. The child is not just significant but the greatest in God's kingdom. The kingdom is not some alternative reality or heaven, but the world as God wants it, as it should be, so this action by Jesus is itself a demonstration of the kingdom in action, with everyone noticing and acknowledging the child. The welcome given to children is the welcome given to Jesus. This must have been astonishing to the adult listeners and difficult to grasp. Why would God want to bring about a world in which the smallest, weakest and most vulnerable are the most privileged? That would not get rid of the Roman occupation or support a powerful Messiah. Yet this is what Jesus tells them is true. God has given all of us a commission to create a world which is fit for children, who are to be welcomed as the first to belong there.

John Pridmore tells the story of going into a school to take an assembly and noticing a child who had fallen asleep. The child was not bored, but exhausted. No one had bothered to put him to bed or to give him breakfast when he got up.[21] For that child to respond to God's commission first to be, and then to respond to God's desire for him, something had to change. That child had been caused to

---

[19] See R. Aasgaard, *My Beloved Brothers and Sisters: Christian Siblingship in Paul* (London: T&T Clark, 2004), p. 38.

[20] Aasgaard, *My Beloved Brothers and Sisters*, p. 50.

[21] J. Pridmore, 'Salvation', in A. Richards and P. Privett, *Through the Eyes of a Child* (London: Church House Publishing, 2009), p. 187.

stumble and Jesus indicts us when at any time we fail to use our God-given abilities to create a world which is fit for children to be privileged, a world in which they can flourish and grow. We may immediately think about children living in poverty or children who run away from home to live on the streets, children who are caught up in crime or children suffering from preventable disease, but what about in our churches?

I was once a member of a large, respected and extremely well-attended church. It was a lively congregation and had many young and enthusiastic families. The vicar, whom I loved dearly, was a gentle, sweet and loving man, but his redoubtable wife was quite another matter. A staunch and devoted supporter of her husband, she could not tolerate anything less than absolute respect for her husband's hard work in preparing his weekly sermon. Consequently, if, when he had made his way into the ancient pulpit and commended his words to God, so much as a squeak emerged from any of the babies and children present in the packed church, what came to be known as the 'Shadow' took action. Without a word, the vicar's wife would rise elegantly from her pew, and silently bear down on the offending child. Still without saying anything she would take the child by the hand or lift the baby from its pram and stalk away, out of the church and back to the vicarage. Amazingly, I never saw a parent object or even try to hold on to their child, but all meekly submitted to the Shadow and her steely glare of reproof. The children were always cared for, played with and happily reunited with the parents afterwards, but these occasions always epitomized for me the way we try to sanitize worship and regulate what happens there. The church was being made fit for well-behaved adults, not for children. The day the vicar preached on 'suffer the little children' while a crying toddler was ejected by the Shadow, always struck me as the supreme irony.

What kind of church really reflects Jesus' kingdom vision of a world which is fit for children? The problem often seems to be that church life and worship is adult driven and oriented and children have to fit in somewhere, rather than entering a place which is fit for them. Many churches get along happily by making accommodation for children, so that they leave the service at a particular time and come back in at another, or are corralled in separate places in the church. Or other churches solve the 'problem' by having specific services for children or at which children are especially welcome. But it does seem difficult to create a worshipping environment in which children are properly at the heart of the vision of God's kingdom in the way Jesus intended.

Some initiatives attempt to deal with the conundrum of what it means to work for God's kingdom made fit for children. Messy Church is an 'attempt to be church for families who might want to meet Jesus, belong to their local church and bring up their children as Christians but can't cope with traditional Sunday morning church services'.[22] Messy Church provides an opportunity for children to be children, playing, exploring within a context of worship and eating together. It offers hospitality, creativity and celebration and is based on the idea of family being at the heart of the encounter with Jesus. Another model is represented by Godly Play[23] which focuses on creating a sacred space in which children can explore their own spiritual leanings at their own pace. Godly Play sessions allow children to wonder and dream about scriptural stories and the adult storyteller attempts to step aside to allow the children to encounter God without hindrance or reinterpretation of their experience. Godly Play is, however, related perhaps more closely to established worship and the rhythms of the Church's year.

Initiatives such as Messy Church and Godly Play both seek in different ways to engage the question of how God calls and commissions children, and many churches have other forms of engagement designed specifically for children. However, the question remains as to how excellent forms of children's engagement and the nourishment of children's spirituality might actually inform and change the Church to make it recognizably a kingdom space that is fit for children. God's calling and commissioning of children, however well nurtured, has to find a place within the calling and commissioning of the family of God, and that is often where a mismatch happens.

I have suggested that one of the problems for many of us is the awkward truth of children's presence and language among us and that the 'Samuel effect' can make worship alongside children a difficult

---

[22] See <www.messychurch.org.uk>.
[23] See <www.godlyplay.org.uk>.

experience. And yet I find that the commission that God offers to children, the 'yes, I am here!' that children offer in response often has a powerful missionary effect on people *outside* the Church, even though people inside may not notice. The power of the school nativity play or children's carol service or Christingle service may reach out and touch unchurched people in ways that we who faithfully attend week by week, year by year, simply do not notice because it is all too familiar. The place of children as real and significant evangelists, in schools, in church and in families, is often overlooked, because their witness emerges naturally from chatter, from play, from making friends and exploring the world together. In order to know ourselves children of God, inheritors of the kingdom, those particular gifts ought to be allowed to shape the Church itself. How that might happen is still, I think, an unanswered question, but unless we pay more attention to it, I don't think we are taking God's own desires for children seriously.

In Chapter 5 I want to return to this challenge in order to consider the lessons of the early Christian church as a community of God's children, a young family, learning to grow in Christ.

Some questions for reflection

- How do you think we can best nurture children's potential and gifts?
- Where do you see children's abilities being stifled or reshaped to what adults want to happen?
- Where in society do you see children being written off if they cannot conform to benchmarks and testing?
- What do *you* imagine Jesus would have been like as a child?

Activity

Try the marshmallow test on a small child (give the child a sweet or a treat and ask him or her not to touch it for fifteen minutes, after which you will let the child have two sweets or treats). What happens? Even if the child fails, give him another sweet or treat anyway. What will you tell the child about why you have done this?

4

God finds children worthy of healing

'Whole . . .'

So far, we have looked at the way God calls new humans into being and how God wants all children to have the opportunity to grow, flourish and to explore their spiritual awareness. We have seen that children have the capacity to respond to God's call with a 'yes!' that allows them to speak God's message to others. We have noted that for these things to happen, there needs to be a suitable context, time and space for children to be nurtured and that such a suitable context is related to God's kingdom reality. I suggested that when children respond to calling and commission others can be challenged and changed in ways which open them to the reconciling and saving acts of God. But in Scripture one of the most powerful forms of witness to God's intention for human beings comes through narratives of healing, when the broken and imperfect world around us is restored and made new.

It's significant then that God finds children worthy of healing. There are two important ways of looking at this. First, how children are the source of healing for others and second, how children themselves are healed and restored. Both these narratives show how suffering, sadness and fear can be changed by God's ways with the world and can show to everyone the divine intent for reconciliation and redemption: the world as it is meant to be. Such events also connect with the eschatological vision of what God wants for the creation, where tears are dried and children come into being and do not die: 'God himself will be with them; he will wipe every tear from their eyes. Death will be no more; mourning and crying and pain will be no more' (Revelation 21.3–4).

The barren woman

In the world of the Bible, infertility spelled disaster. Without children who could survive to adulthood, the family name could not be carried on, the people-group could not flourish and the community could not survive. Moreover, God's desire for the community was that it should be 'fruitful and multiply' so barrenness could also be associated with sinfulness. Infertility was therefore seen as a visible sign within the religious community that something was deeply wrong with the world.

At the heart of this was a focus on the way God has disposed the creation. Human beings are sexually reproducing creatures and heterosexual sex results in the conception and birth of children. It is not surprising then that some other forms of sexual practice, which cannot lead to procreation, are described as contrary to God's intention for human beings.[1] However, there is more to it than this, because the prevalent idiom in the Hebrew Scripture for conception through sexual intercourse, involves the direct action of God. God is said to 'open' or 'close' the wombs of women. This striking phrase has a number of important resonances. First, it echoes what we said in Chapter 1 about how God gets his hands dirty with the evolution and outworking of human biology. Second, it implies that despite the expulsion from Eden, God continues to be at work in the creation of new life inside human bodies. God 'opens the womb' in order to enable that calling into being that is at the heart of creation and is present at the conception of a new human being made in God's image. Third, the opening of the womb implies the intimacy and closeness of the 'one flesh' in the act of sex. The womb is opened so that the new child may begin his or her life. Consequently, sex acts in which the opening/closing of the womb is not an option effectively leave the Creator outside human intimacy and in fact create the barrenness of which the biblical communities are so afraid. In the world of the Bible, a society in which procreation is deliberately defeated or is not an issue in the expression of love and desire between individuals, cannot be imagined.

---

[1] This is not the same as saying categorically that this or that sexual practice is outlawed by God for ever, any more than we can say that heterosexual sex in a time and place far removed from the world of the Bible ceases to have core relevance. The issue is rather a question of what is the adult human body, and the capacity for sex *for*, in a specific context where only heterosexual practice resulting in children results in benefit to the beleaguered tribe in a dangerous world. On the other hand, the issue of what the adult human body and the capacity for sex is *for*, is still a critical question and has to be re-asked with rigour in each generation against the social construction of the societies in which we live.

Barrenness is not just about the inability of the woman to conceive or bear children. The idea of the closing of the womb may also imply impotence on behalf of the husband, though perhaps understandably in a patriarchal society that would not be a popular subject.[2] It would be easier to blame God. We may perhaps hear this in Rachel's plea to Jacob: 'Give me sons, for if you don't, I'm a dead woman! And Jacob was incensed with Rachel, and he said "Am I instead of God, Who has denied you fruit of the womb?"' (Genesis 30.1–2).[3] Customs and laws were put in place to ensure that fertile women were given suitable chances to have children, hence the requirement that if a man died, his unmarried brother should marry her (levirate marriage).

Barrenness in the Bible, then, creates a situation within the family in which God's purposes and the social purposes of the community are thwarted. This raises the issue of both stigma and blame – what has a person done wrong to deserve this? It can be seen as a curse laid on a family for disobedience towards God (see Deuteronomy 28.28). But the suffering of women who want to become pregnant but cannot comes across clearly in a number of places in the Scriptures. The barren woman is 'desolate' (Isaiah 54.1), filled with 'distress' and 'misery' (1 Samuel 1.10–11), a source of shame (Genesis 30.23), and a 'disgrace' (Luke 1.25). Duty, honour, shame and religious impropriety swirl around the perplexing issue of why a marriage is not fruitful (the typical epithet for a child is 'fruit of the womb') and a common human solution in the Hebrew Scriptures is for a husband to have children by a concubine or slave-girl instead. We see this with Abraham and Hagar and also with Rachel's slave-girl Bilhah, whom Rachel wants to give birth 'on my knees' so that Rachel can vicariously give birth. Leah, similarly, believing that she won't have any more children gives her slave-girl, Zilpah, to Jacob, although Leah goes on to have more children after all (Genesis 30.9–21).

Yet beyond the problems and solutions of fertility and childbearing in these ancient societies, another theological strand emerges. God, who opens and closes the womb, reacts to the distress and pain

---

[2] See R. Alter, *The Five Books of Moses* (New York: W. W. Norton, 2004), p. 101 note 18 about male impotence in Genesis 20—21.

[3] Alter, *The Five Books of Moses*, pp. 158–9.

of those who want to bear children, often in miraculous and unexpected ways. In fact, for people who are fertile and have families
without difficulty, the extraordinary power of God might actually
pass them by. It is in the lives of the distressed women in barren
relationships that people become more spiritually aware and that
God can be seen to be dynamically at work. The usual phrase is
that 'God hears' the distress of the barren woman and 'heals' her
with a child. The psalmist, for example, praises God for caring for
the needy and vulnerable and raising them up, adding that 'He seats
the barren woman in her home a happy mother of sons. Hallelujah'
(Psalm 113.9).[4] The writer of Isaiah 54.1 also imagines Israel's recovery
as the praise and thanksgiving of barren women who are healed
by pregnancy: 'Sing, O barren one who did not bear; burst into song
and shout, you who have not been in labour! For the children
of the desolate woman will be more than the children of her that is
married, says the LORD.'[5] That healing has a number of important
elements which we can unpack.

Because God gets his hands dirty with our biology, God's actions
can make possible what is apparently impossible. It is a fact of biology
that conception may become more difficult as a woman ages, so
both Sarah who 'no longer had her woman's flow'[6] and the aged
Elizabeth (Luke 1.7) do not expect ever to become pregnant.[7] In both
these cases the advanced age of the husband is also represented as
a factor. The very idea that Sarah could have sex and conceive seems
mad to her and she laughs in disbelief at the suggestion. Yet God
is able to heal the ravages of time with a pregnancy. Why does God
do this?

We are told that God hears the misery and suffering of women
who desire to become pregnant and cannot. When God hears the
distressed voices of such people, he responds, so the barren woman
now appears alongside the needy, the vulnerable, the widow and the
aged in God's economy. Those at the bottom of the heap, shamed,

---

[4] R. Alter, *The Book of Psalms* (New York: W. W. Norton, 2007), p. 403.

[5] See also the use of this passage in Galatians 4.27 in the allegory about Hagar and Sarah.

[6] Alter, *The Five Books of Moses*, p. 87.

[7] The writer of Luke carefully inserts that both Elizabeth and Zechariah were 'righteous before God,
living blamelessly according to all the commandments and regulations of the Lord' (Luke 1.6),
perhaps in order to separate them from the question – what did they do to deserve this?

dishonoured, rejected, or lost in the system are the ones who are heard and also healed, their pride and social status restored. As they fall to the bottom of the heap, God's option for those in most need becomes effective. In the case of the barren women, these social and psychic wounds are healed with a child. No one can now look with disfavour on her or ask what sin she or her family has committed, since God has given her the fruit of her womb.

Further, in the cases where the barren woman has been heard by God and healed by an unexpected pregnancy, the message is reinforced by a promise of the significance of the child to the life of the community. The woman's suffering is compensated not just by the longed-for pregnancy but by the importance of the child in the future of the nation. So the cry to God from the barren woman is greeted by an abundance of grace. It is not surprising then that many of these promises of a child are given as prophetic announcements – by an angel, a priest or a prophet. This is very important, because it makes the healing of the unfulfilled family a matter of a sacred space in which God's intention and purpose for the world as a good place for humans to flourish is made clear.

How does this prophetic, God-filled space work? It seems to operate by expanding human horizons through both time and space, and thus provides a glimpse of God's perspective. From a human point of view, human ageing and death offer a limited horizon in which desires and intentions are limited and not all can be fulfilled, but in the healing of barren women God opens up a limitless perspective. With the birth of Isaac to Sarah, God promises that 'I will establish My covenant with him as an everlasting covenant, for his seed after him' (Genesis 17.19)[8] and for Abraham's son Ishmael, conceived in response to barrenness, 'I will make him a great nation' (Genesis 17.20). Similarly,

> There was a certain man of Zorah, of the tribe of the Danites, whose name was Manoah. His wife was barren, having borne no children. And the angel of the LORD appeared to the woman and said to her, 'Although you are barren, having borne no children, you shall conceive and bear a son. Now be careful not to drink wine or strong drink, or to eat anything unclean, for you shall conceive and bear a son. No

---

[8] Alter, *The Five Books of Moses*, p. 84.

razor is to come on his head, for the boy shall be a nazirite to God from birth. It is he who shall begin to deliver Israel from the hand of the Philistines.' (Judges 13.2–5)

This child is Samson. What is interesting here is that the healing of the woman's barrenness with a child is accompanied by a concern for the health of the pregnant woman and her child. Although the woman is not named, she is to take care of herself. This divine care for the pregnant woman does not guarantee a life of continuing joy, however – Samson's life wreaking bloody havoc on the Philistines must have caused his parents continuing concern. Similarly, the annunciation to Mary, not a barren woman but an unmarried young woman, comes with an announcement of an extraordinary future, which will change the world for ever, but is later supplemented with another prophetic note, 'a sword will pierce your heart'. Healing is not the same as, and does not guarantee, happiness.

Notwithstanding, the recognition and delight of women who have unexpectedly been granted a child can pour out. We see this in the Song of Hannah and the Song of Mary, which echo each other.

Hannah gives her longed-for son Samuel into God's service in gratitude to God for hearing her prayer, and she says:

> My heart exults in the LORD;
> my strength is exalted in my God.
> My mouth derides my enemies,
> because I rejoice in my victory . . .
> The barren has borne seven,
> but she who has many children is forlorn.
> The LORD kills and brings to life . . .
> he brings low, he also exalts.
> (1 Samuel 2.1, 5, 7)

This comes across as an utterance of joy. There is a healing from the shame and stigma of childlessness and the person is raised up within the community. This reversal of fortune, however, happens in a sacred space and is recognized as an act of God who is working to establish a world in which people are lifted up from the bottom of the heap. So the child has more than a personal or even community significance. The child has a cosmic significance in that he heals a major rift in the way God wants the world to be. It is not surprising then that Mary's Magnificat contains the same vocabulary and sentiments. Jesus too is coming into the world to establish God's kingdom. The Gospel writers surround Jesus' infancy narrative with events which connect this miraculous birth with its vast significance. The angel announces 'good news of great joy' (Luke 2.10) for everyone and promises God's favour and peace to the shepherds. The magi follow a sign in the sky (Matthew 2.2). Simeon, on seeing the child Jesus in the Temple, praises God and announces that in Jesus there is 'salvation, which you have prepared in the presence of all the peoples, a light for revelation to the Gentiles and for glory to your people Israel' (Luke 2.30–32). An elderly woman called Anna sees Jesus, praises God and tells everyone 'looking for the redemption of Jerusalem' about the child who has been born (Luke 2.36–38). And, most magisterially, the opening of John's Gospel gives us the testimony of the meaning of the child's birth directly, as a healing for the whole universe: 'the true light, which enlightens everyone, was coming into the world' (John 1.9).

The important principle then is that children are given through God's grace to women who have not been able to conceive, but that local reversal of fortune means much, much more. Through such occurrences, God's divine will is revealed: things can and must change for the better. The healing of a physical, social hurt through the gift of a child teaches us about the much larger reconciling and healing purposes of God. Despite the fact that the world seems unfair and biased and just wrong much of the time, the inhabiting of a sacred space in which the divine message of peace and goodwill can come through is made concrete in the birth of children.

How does this help *us*?

We have said that Scripture shows us ways in which God is intimately involved with the coming into being of children, that God is intimately involved in the way the human biology of sex operates and that God is, at significant moments, intimately involved in the healing of those who desire children but who have not been able to have them. That healing is marked by the gift of a child, even a special child, but while that healing carries a much larger significance about what God is doing with the world, that is no guarantor of happiness or fulfilment for the individual parents. Simeon warns Mary that 'a sword will pierce your own soul too' (Luke 2.35). What does any of this have to say to people who want children but who are facing infertility in today's world?

I once had a friend who got married and went off happily on her honeymoon. When she and her husband returned her parents-in-law came to stay with the newlyweds. My friend's mother-in-law took her aside and showed her a scrapbook in which had been posted pictures of the wedding and little keepsakes. But in the middle of the scrapbook was a blank page with only a title. It said 'Grandchildren'.

My friend and her husband had assumed that in the fullness of time they would have a family, but they had reckoned without the mother-in-law. It didn't help that her other son and daughter had already produced a number of grandchildren whose photos and exploits filled a number of bulging scrapbooks. On every visit, the mother-in-law produced the empty scrapbook with its uninhabited pages as a silent, but effective rebuke. Phone calls from the mother to the son started, 'Is she pregnant yet?'

Time passed. My friend decided that she and her husband would try for a baby even though neither was convinced they were ready. Sex became a chore, and failure each month a source of sadness and recrimination. The mother-in-law even started to hint darkly that the empty pages were caused by some ineradicable biological fault in my friend and that her son should think about divorce. Everyone became more and more unhappy. Eventually the couple went for fertility treatment, but my friend confided to me that she felt more like an incubator and that any child could never really be hers because everyone else in the family was so invested in owning it. She finally conceived and had a miscarriage which led to further recriminations and bitterness. The marriage ended. Later she remarried and had a healthy child.

How does what we learn from Scripture help us react to a story like this? The stigma and failure associated with childlessness are present, as is the pressure to ensure the continuation of the family, but here the 'healing' that a child would bring only appears to satisfy the mother-in-law. The child becomes a bargaining counter, a source of resentment, causing the widening of a rift in the relationships and actually being a means of damage to the marriage. 'Treatment' for the infertility only solves the problem of external pressure from the mother-in-law and her accusatory scrapbook; the wider meaning of release from barrenness is missing.

So one of the things we can take from Scripture is that healing from barrenness needs *necessarily* to be accompanied by the song of thanksgiving and joy that Scripture reports from Hannah and Mary. That song is not just a one-off event, however, but a continuing melody in which the presence of children demonstrates to us something about God's vision for the future. If bringing children into the world means misery, suffering, recrimination and anxiety, then something has gone wrong with what God wants for the lives of those children and the 'healing' is eclipsed or missing. We have to hear the song and know that it is both genuine and long-lasting, for God's vision to come near. That means that those things which eclipse the song of joy: post-partum depression, economic hardship, the struggle to find adequate and affordable carers, these are things which urgently need attention if we are to build a world fit for children.

On an even larger scale, we have to ask how we can generally understand what God wants for the lives of children when we look at the healing of infertility today. This is a complex task which requires a great deal of thought because the world we inhabit now looks and feels very different from the world of the Bible. Our planet is overpopulated with human beings who in order to live consume vast numbers of resources, damaging the environment and the habitats of other living creatures and condemning many people to lives of poverty and malnutrition. We also live in a world where we know a great deal about what happens in the process of sex, and what is required for conception. So much so, in fact, that we today have the capability to take eggs and sperm from people's bodies and freeze them. We can create embryo humans and implant them later. We can screen these embryos to find out their sex and their genetic makeup. We can implant those embryos in the womb of the mother or in the womb of another woman altogether. We can choose which embryos make a person pregnant, raising the possibility of so-called 'saviour siblings' and 'designer' children. We even have situations where a transgendered person born as a woman but living as a man can become pregnant, where women well past the menopause can conceive,[9] where two women or two men living as partners can arrange for a pregnancy to take place and for the child to thereafter have two mothers or two fathers. We also live in a world where reliable contraception means that pregnancy can be avoided altogether and where two people who are regularly having sex can expect, if they wish, to remain voluntarily childless for the duration of their lives. Indeed voluntary childlessness, free from the social stigmas of the biblical world, might today mean that we should have a greater appreciation for the loving role of others besides parents in children's lives. Where today do we hear the songs of Hannah and Mary? Is it in the clinic, is it in the homes of gay or lesbian couples? Is it sung by sisters and brothers and aunts and uncles who have decided not to have children of their own but who love and nurture other children of the family? Are these different songs or the same song?

I think it is very important that we listen closely to the different songs we now hear. Scripture, of course, simply does not envisage such a world of technological advance, variety of sexual relationships and choice and decision-making within those relationships. Scripture is silent, for example, on issues like voluntary childlessness, the closest issue being the 'sin' of Onan who took steps during sex not to impregnate his partner. We cannot 'make' Scripture offer us information about matters which are beyond the scope of the lives of the human beings who inhabit its stories. But there should still be some basic principles about God's relation to children that do not change.

The first, I think, is that having a child is an essential good which echoes the goodness of the creation, but even in Scripture children are not born into a vacuum. Children are born into the world, and there has to be an understanding that the world is part of the deal. God cares for women, for pregnant women, for children and for the world they inhabit. So if we have got to the point where the world cannot sustain the children we bring into it, we have strayed away

---

[9] B. Marsh, 'Dozens of Babies being Born to Mothers over Fifty', *Daily Telegraph* 8 May 2006, online at <www.telegraph.co.uk/news/uknews/3339190/Dozens-of-babies-being-born-to-mothers-over-50>.

from God's purposes and intention. We have to consider the world and the environment into which the child is born. That world can be geographical, societal, familial. Having children should be good for the world, not bad for it. God's gifts to the barren women are healing influences, not burdens.

The second is that no matter how good our technology, we can't get away from the fact that human biology has not changed. Children can only come about through a meeting of sperm and egg and women's and men's fertility is still affected by biological age. There is something very particular and fundamental about heterosexual sex and the nature of human reproduction. That's not to say that fertility treatment is intrinsically bad, but people who go through cycles of IVF can sometimes feel that something important is lost. Some of my friends have talked about the unpleasantness of the clinical nature of IVF – the collecting of samples is a long way from the closeness and intimacy of trying for a baby together. Similarly, things that we *can* do, such as surrogacy or gamete donation, which add to the number of people directly or indirectly involved in a pregnancy, test our notions of what the healing gift of a child actually means in today's technologically advanced society.[10] Perhaps we need to find ways of bringing a consciousness of God's role back into this: a hope of joyful healing rather than treatment of a problem.

Third, we need to hold on to the sense of precious gift that is experienced by the formerly barren when we think about infertility questions in a world like ours. Infertility treatment offers hope and joy to many couples who want children but have trouble conceiving naturally, but in cases where treatments might take place for the aggrandizement of scientific advance, personal preference, to 'cheat' ageing, or to fulfil the 'right' to a child, there is clearly a movement away from the idea of the child as a gracious and precious gift to one of the child as a paid-for object or commodity which tells us about the mechanisms of human will but nothing of divine import. In the story of my friend's initial infertility, earlier in this chapter, other

---

[10] Useful information to help us think about these complex matters is available from the Church of England's website at <www.churchofengland.org/our-views/medical-ethics-health-social-care-policy.aspx>; or look at K. O'Rourke and P. Boyle, *Medical Ethics: Sources of Catholic Teachings* (Washington: Georgetown University Press, 4th edn 2011); N. Messer, *Respecting Life: Theology and Bioethics* (London: SCM Press, 2011).

people in the family were turning her future child into a commodity to be owned and exploited, not a new person to be cherished.

Christian ethics offer ways into thinking about these issues, but I want to keep hold of our focus on the child at the heart of it all, whose presence, through the agency of God, is intended to bring healing into hurt families. Then it makes perfect sense that God should seek to heal the whole world by sending his own Son, as a child, to live and grow among human beings. Keeping that focus helps us realize that it is not a question of what Scripture tells us to do, but what Scripture makes it clear we should not lose sight of, not forget. One of those things is the song of joy that issues from the mouth of the woman whose prayer has been heard and which is sealed in the presence of her child. Another is that the presence of the precious child in the world is a sign of the reality of God's reconciling work for the whole creation.

Barrenness revisited

Yet despite our current increased understanding and the technology available to treat infertility, there are still many for whom the womb remains obstinately 'closed' and for whom the song of parental joy remains elusive throughout life. Does that mean that there is no healing for them? Are such people not found worthy by God of receiving the healing presence of a child? The answer goes back to what I discussed in Chapter 1 about the varied nature of our biology. God calls every child to be, but some never make it because their bodies are not formed properly. Similarly, for some men and women, their bodies, for whatever reasons, do not allow them to initiate pregnancies or perhaps to bear children, or to give birth to children who can survive. Medicine and scientific research continues to address such problems, but as with all such complex issues, not all such problems have a remedy.[11] Yet we can say with confidence that God continues to find people worthy of call and healing no matter what circumstances get in the way of that vision being realized. That is why God tirelessly reconciles the world to himself

---

[11] Support and help for these problems is offered by charities such as <www.miscarriageassociation. org.uk>; <www.infertilitynetworkuk.com>; <www.malefertility.co.uk>.

(2 Corinthians 5.19) and enjoins us to be partners with the divine vision to make that reconciliation a reality. I won't pretend that that kind of language is going to comfort one of my friends who has just suffered a fourth miscarriage and at whose side I have nothing to offer but tears for her grief, but for some people, the confidence that God sees in them the possibility of being carers of children, despite physical difficulties, can sometimes show people, who cannot have children of their own, pathways to being beloved teachers, carers, or adoptive parents of other children, not their own, who need their care and protection.

Sick children can be healed

In the second film of *The Lord of the Rings*, grieving King Théoden, played by Bernard Hill, speaks for all parents in the developed world when he says that 'no parent should have to bury their child'. Yet this is a very modern thing to say. I once visited a town where the church gravestones had been arranged around the perimeter of a public park and, lined up like this, it was very easy to read the history of death in a close community. The story of the gravestones showed that only a hundred years or so ago, many children were wiped out by diseases like influenza or consumption (tuberculosis) and families often lost all their children, sometimes within days. With comprehensive vaccination against common childhood diseases like measles and whooping cough, better diet and living conditions, to lose a child to illness in the western world is much more rare and the more shocking because unexpected. In other parts of the world, of course, it is a different story and families still lose large numbers of children to malnutrition, malaria, AIDS, dysentery and cholera, among other terrible diseases.

What, then, drives our contemporary attitudes to the sickness and death of children? One story may help to get at the heart of this. In October 2011 an inquest was held into the death of a four-month-old baby boy. The baby had died of meningitis in Basildon hospital in Essex in 2008, but on the day he died, his young mother had taken him to her local health centre three times. The baby was seen by a doctor, a nurse practitioner and the doctor again before the child's grandmother called an ambulance. The baby died shortly afterwards.

The mother had questioned whether her baby should have been referred to hospital sooner by the doctor and whether that would have saved his life. After hearing evidence the coroner accepted from a paediatric expert that the aggressive nature of the disease was such that the baby might have been beyond saving even before the classic signs of meningitis appeared and that even if he had gone to hospital sooner the doctors there might not have diagnosed meningitis. The coroner, accepting this, therefore ruled that the baby died of natural causes.[12]

This tragic story is worthy of further reflection. If we look deeper into the various points of view we can see the issues which are at the heart of how we feel about sick children. In the first instance there is the mother who just *knows* there is something terribly wrong with her baby. She turns for advice to *her* mother, and as the day wears on, we can imagine their fear and distress as the baby becomes progressively and rapidly more ill. For them, there is a trade-off between being reassured by the calm professionalism of a doctor and the nurse, and their own instincts that the baby is much more dangerously ill which brings them back twice to the health centre. Finally, their faith in the health system breaks down and the grand-mother calls an ambulance, but it is too late.

On the other side of the coin, doctors see worried and fretful parents all the time. A child with a fever who appears listless and ill may simply have a cold. Doctors have to sift through the parent's agitation, worry and distress to check for danger signs and if they are not present, reassure the parent and give advice on how to manage the sick child. Doctors also have to consider that if a child is sent to hospital, this will be very worrying and frightening and the child may still be sent home after all. On the other hand, children with meningitis can die very quickly, as in this case. Yet again, if caught quickly, meningitis is treatable.

There can be other issues too. If doctors can be proved negligent, they can be sued for financial compensation and sometimes that is a factor in the question of whether a person could or should have been healed.

---

[12] L. Kirby, 'Mum's Questions over Tot's Death', *Thurrock Gazette*, 14 October 2011, p. 5, and 'Tot Inquest Ruling', *Thurrock Gazette*, 21 October 2011, p. 4.

The inquest had to test the question: was everything that could be done, actually done? The coroner's view was that nothing else would have made a difference; effectively the baby was doomed as soon as he got ill. That is the way of the world: children sometimes get so sick, they die.

But it is not simply a matter of where the baby fell in the medical system. There are deeper questions too about why *this* child? What an inquest will not expose is who we look to and trust when our children are ill. Is it the mother's gut instinct that there is something terribly wrong? Is it professionals who are supposed to look on the child and draw from their wealth of experience and training the knowledge and wisdom to know what the next steps are? Will we suppress one in favour of the other? And do we assume that somehow, someone *must* know what the best course of action is? In addition, the story does not tell us about the powerful search for meaning and the intense feelings of guilt which attend a sick child. Am I doing the right thing? What else should I do? The story does not communicate the feelings of helplessness, hope and fear, when a person hands over his or her sick child into the care of others. Who should be blamed afterwards – should we try to blame the medical professionals to deflect the guilt we feel ourselves? Will it help if the coroner says it is no one's fault? Can all the questions surrounding a child's death be answered, and finally, who actually *cared* that the child suffered and died?

These elements of the story lead us more deeply into the spiritual realms. How can we know what God wants in any of this? Where is God in the lives and deaths of children and how is God's purpose worked out in how and why that happens?

The scriptural background is unsurprisingly very different from our modern world of healthcare and hospitals. Indeed, what we see is a world in which children suffer and die *en masse*. As we have already seen, disease, famine and hardship take their toll on the weak and the vulnerable and so voices from Scripture arise full of lamentation and grief for dead children.

Yet out of this background, so very similar to the stories of death and disease which come from other parts of the world still today, are a few stories which absolutely stand out in the sense that we learn from them so much about how God finds children worthy of healing. We can find a number of important stories where children are at the point of death and something extraordinary happens, something that can leave us with new knowledge about God and what God wants for the lives of children.

Elijah and the widow's son

One story which helps us understand this is recounted in 1 Kings 17. This is the beginning of the story of the prophet Elijah and the material, which probably had an introduction which is now lost, dramatically emphasizes the power of God throughout. Further, it is necessary to remember that the Deuteronomistic theologians who put the material together probably laced together the healing story with other sections to create the dramatic continuous narrative we read in the Bible.[13] The context requires us to plunge into an immediate danger and threat to survival for everyone – Elijah tells King Ahab that there will be no rain. There is a severe drought and Elijah himself is in imminent peril, yet submission to God sustains his life. God tells him where to hide and by following God's word, Elijah is able to drink the little water that remains in a wadi and ravens provide him with food. Yet the wadi still dries up and Elijah is likely to die. God next directs him to Zarephath in Sidon on the Phoenician coast, where he will find a widow to feed him. When he arrives, Elijah indeed finds a poor widow but she too is living at the edge of subsistence. How can they survive? Another miracle occurs: the tiny amount of food the widow has holds out to feed not only Elijah but also the widow and her family 'for many days'.

This, then, is the context: a desperate attempt to stay alive in a foreign land without water, among the poor who are running out of food. Now there is a further calamity, the widow's son becomes desperately ill and is dead or at death's door: 'there was no breath left in him'. The widow is distraught and blames Elijah. But Elijah takes the child from her, carries him to his room, asks God why this disaster has happened and effects a healing ritual in which he stretches out on the child, while praying to God to let the child

---

[13] See J. Barton and J. Muddiman, *The Oxford Bible Commentary* (Oxford: Oxford University Press, 2001), p. 245.

live. God hears Elijah's prayer and the child revives. Elijah brings the child down and gives him back to his mother.[14]

The story as it is told also gives us some other insights. First, the context of the healing is extraordinarily intimate. The child is taken from his mother's breast and held close by Elijah. In the prophet's room, Elijah 'stretches out' on the child. This might be a primitive form of chest compression[15] restarting the child's heart, or it might be that we are meant to understand that the prophet breathes into the child's nostrils in a copy of God's animation of the dust which led to the creation of Adam. In either case, what Elijah does is extraordinary. He is the prophet of God, employed on God's business, who intervenes powerfully, intimately, in order to save the life of a child who is not even from his own people. This is all done in the arena of the prophet's relationship and dialogue with God. The cry to God about the death of the child and the plea to God to allow the child to live are rewarded with the restoration of the child. Yet this is not a matter of Elijah leaving God to effect a miracle out of thin air. Elijah has to act, to be a dynamic force in the effort of trying to save the child, to be the difference between life and death. The outcome is also important in another way: when Elijah restores the child to his mother, she recognizes both the validity of Elijah's own vocation and believes in the God of Israel: 'the word of the LORD in your mouth is truth' (1 Kings 17.24). So the healing of the child creates a new space in which meaning and purpose are revealed.

Elisha and the raising of the Shunnamite's son

Alongside this story we can also look at its parallel in 2 Kings 4.18–37. Various elements are very close to the story of Elijah, including the

---

[14] The Babylonian Talmud (Sanhedrin 113a) gives us an interesting insight into thinking about why the story of the drought and the saving of the child are put together. God is depicted as holding three keys, one for birth, one for rain and one for resurrection. Elijah already has the key for rain as indicated by his ability to tell Ahab that there will be drought. But now with the widow's son he is also asking for the key of resurrection. To have both would mean he had more keys (and powers) than God, so he has to give the rain key back if he is to save the widow's son. So Elijah gives the rain key back and uses the key of resurrection to bring the child back to life. The general issue of demonstrating God's power over an entire territory is sacrificed to the particular: the healing of a child.

[15] See J. Gwilt, 'Biblical Ills and Remedies', *Journal of the Royal Society of Medicine* 79.12 (1986), pp. 738–41.

miracle of the oil, the making of a room in the house for the prophet and the healing of a child, but here the text is at pains to express the preciousness of the child to the woman. She is originally barren, but Elisha prophesies that she will have a son and indeed she does. But disaster strikes and the child cries out 'Oh my head, my head!' His mother cuddles him on her lap, but he dies. The woman then takes the child and lays him on Elisha's bed and goes to look for the prophet. She clutches him in her distress and while his servant tries to pull her away, Elisha takes pity on her. Elisha tells his servant to go to the house urgently and lay his staff on the child's face. The servant does so but reports that the child does not wake up. Elisha then prays to God and lies on the child to resuscitate him and the child revives: 'the flesh of the child became warm' (2 Kings 4.34). It takes a little while for the child to revive properly but when he does, Elisha restores him to his mother.

From this parallel story we are invited to enter the drama and fear of the situation, as we might react to any one of our children who comes in crying out 'my head, my head!' The mother's instinct is to hold the child and comfort him but when he is obviously beyond such help she goes to even greater lengths, saddling her donkey and riding out in a desperate dash to get to the only source of help she knows. Despite being restrained, she gets through to Elisha and enlists his aid, but the situation seems hopeless. Yet again, the narrative offers us a picture of powerful intimate healing ritual, twinning Elisha's living body with the child's dead one and revivifying him, effectively giving him mouth-to-mouth resuscitation in terms of breathing his spirit (or breath) into the child's body. Once again, the act of doing something is set in the context of prayer and an appeal to God's power and will for the child.

Taking these two stories together, we can see certain significant elements in understanding what Scripture says about how God finds children worthy of healing. There is a small personal tragedy in the midst of greater events, but even that one life, a child's life, is found worthy of God's attention and a wholehearted effort to heal a child. Further, love and nurture surround the healing. The boy's mother in the Elisha story holds and comforts her son and in both cases, Elijah and Elisha deal with the children in the privacy and sanctity of their rooms. The intimacy and personal investment in the healing is a long way from Elijah's very public contest with the priests of Baal. The healings themselves take place in the context of prayer and in submission to God's will and require not only touch (overcoming prohibitions against touching dead bodies which will make a person unclean) but a giving of the whole physical self in an attempt to bring the child back. The parallels with the primordial act of creation are important, because God's fundamental acts of creation are not just good but good for ever. If the broken, fallen world threatens that fundamental reality, then the creative act can be reinvoked to restore it. God wants this. Both Elijah and Elisha hold nothing back, but give of their whole physical and spiritual being in order to allow the power of God to work a healing miracle. The outcome of the healings are also important: through the restoration of the child's life and the giving back of the child to the mother, the truth of God's desire and promise for human beings is made known.

The healing of Jairus' daughter

The background of the narrative parallel healings of children by Elijah and Elisha is important when we come to examine the healing of Jairus' daughter by Jesus as recounted in Mark 5.21–43. We know from Luke 4 that Jesus explicitly refers to Elijah's miracles in relation to the widow of Zarephath, because as he announces his ministry, Jesus says that God's power was particularly made manifest outside the Jewish community and it was a foreign woman whose son was restored and who believed as a result. Jesus was steeped in that extraordinary story and we can keep it in mind as we consider what happens in two important healing miracles, the healing of the Syro-Phoenician woman's daughter and the story of Jairus' daughter.

The narrative begins with Jairus, a leader of the synagogue, prostrating himself at the feet of Jesus as the Shunnamite woman did at the feet of Elisha. His errand is the same: his daughter is at the 'point of death' and he implores Jesus to go to her and heal her. There is no doubt in Jairus' mind that Jesus can do this: 'Come and lay your hands on her, so that she may be made well, and live' (v. 23). Jairus expects that Jesus will heal by touch, as in the prophet's healings and Jesus' own practice.

At this point Mark presents an intercalation: an interweaving of another dramatic story. A suffering woman, who has exhausted all her resources on doctors without result, comes to Jesus as her last resort. She makes her way to Jesus and instead of asking for his healing touch, is satisfied that if she can just touch him herself, then she will be healed of her haemorrhaging (presumably menorrhagia). Yet just as this story cuts through the narrative of Jairus' daughter, at the point when Jesus is making his way to Jairus' house, tension rises in our minds about the fate of the child and the desperation of her father. Jesus must get there as soon as possible or she will die. Yet Jesus stops, searching the crowd for the woman and somehow knowing that 'power' has gone out of him to heal another person. The woman comes to him and confesses what she has done and that she is healed. Jesus confirms her faith and her healing and sends her away with his blessing. Immediately, it seems that the woman has effectively ended the life of the child and claimed the healing miracle for herself. News comes that the child has died and it is suggested that there is no longer any point wasting Jesus' time on a hopeless quest. But Jesus insists on taking a few disciples, losing the crowd and continuing to Jairus' house. Once there, the mourners are already swinging into action. Jesus suggests that despite what everyone says, there is still hope for those with faith, but everyone laughs at him. The next part of the narrative bears close attention:

> Then he put them all outside, and took the child's father and mother and those who were with him, and went in where the child was. He took her by the hand and said to her, 'Talitha cum', which means 'Little girl, get up!' And immediately the girl got up and began to walk about (she was twelve years of age). At this they were overcome with amazement. He strictly ordered them that no one should know this, and told them to give her something to eat.   (Mark 5.40–43)

As in the Elijah and Elisha examples, Jesus heals the child in private with her family and a few chosen disciples as witnesses. The healing itself is both intimate, entailing physically touching the child, and tender. The words Jesus uses are given to us as a command, and are given in Aramaic, so that we are invited to hear Jesus' words, but the text does not perhaps catch the intimacy of the moment. Talitha is translated 'little girl' but Geza Vermes has suggested the original meaning is closer to 'little kid' (i.e. little goat), a more personal address specifically for a child.[16] The child immediately responds to Jesus' voice and gets up. Jesus instructs both the parents and the disciples that the details of the miracle must be kept quiet, and that the child must be cared for and nurtured.

This account has obvious links with the Elijah/Elisha story, but through what Jesus does in Mark's account we can learn even more about how God finds children worthy of healing. First, once Jairus has asked for help, nothing stops Jesus from getting through to his daughter, despite interruptions, a crowd pressing on him from every side, a usurpation of his healing power by another, and the news that the child is beyond help anyway.[17] *Nothing* stops Jesus from seeking out, coming to and healing the little girl. Despite having very little 'worth' in the human social and economic terms of that time, being a child, female and dead, yet Jesus finds in her something of complete value, worthy of saving and healing, loved by God, not least because she is loved by her father to whom Jesus responds.

Another significant feature of this healing is the way that Jesus carries it out in private and by direct engagement with the child without reference to anyone else, parents included. As with Elijah/ Elisha, the healing is carried out by direct physical contact. But this child is not male but female, involving a cutting through taboos about touching female or dead bodies. Moreover the healing is by direct speech to the child herself, addressed to the child *as a child*, and resulting in a restoration of life, health (she begins to walk about) and relationship (she is restored to her parents who are to feed and care for her). Jesus not only finds the child worthy of healing but makes provision for her future welfare; she is to grow and be nourished and to become what God desires for her.

---

[16] G. Vermes, *The Authentic Gospel of Jesus* (London: The Folio Society, 2009 [2003]), p. 11.

[17] It is sometimes suggested that the narrative works like this to show Jesus delaying so that the child will have died by the time he gets to her. I certainly think that time matters in Mark's Gospel. However, I also think that for Jesus and the healing power of God time is immaterial. It does not matter that in human terms Jesus is 'too late' to get to Lazarus and to Jairus' daughter; what Jesus' actions show is that our experience of time is not a factor in God's reconciling and healing work. Once Jesus has agreed to come to Jairus' daughter, nothing will stop the healing from taking place. Again, I think that we can extrapolate from how God finds this child worthy of healing, to God's desire that all should be healed, restored and saved.

Further, we should not forget about the woman with the flow of blood. The intercalation is not just there for dramatic effect, although it certainly serves that purpose. There are clear links between the child and the woman. The child is about twelve and presumably around the point of puberty and the beginning of menstruation; the woman has suffered from her haemorrhaging for about the same amount of time. The child is Jairus' daughter; Jesus addresses the woman as 'daughter'. What does this connection mean?

One way of looking at it is to see the woman who is healed as another potential picture of the child in later life. Jesus does not just heal a person at a specific place and time, the healing goes deeper than that: what God wants is for a person to be whole and healed for his or her entire life. God does not stop wanting that person to flourish, grow and be healthy. Obviously it is the way of the world that people do suffer and die, but the point of healing is to make it possible for that person to have a future that glorifies God. That is why Jesus calls to the child and asks the parents to take care of her. It is not then a case of leaving her to manage on her own. God will be there throughout her life and if things go wrong, Jesus is still always available and her faith can make her well. In the two pictures of the child and the woman we can see the entire span of a woman's reproductive life from beginning to menopause.

This is even more extraordinary when we consider the range of Jewish rituals and laws regarding female bodies and their functions. Yet these matters, wound round with custom, purity issues and taboo, come right into the heart of Jesus' ministry. Imagine the state the poor woman must have been in and how difficult her life must have been if she was bleeding copiously for years. Yet Jesus not only accepts her, but heals her in this most intimate of female conditions. We are asked then to think about the child's future, and we know she is going to be all right no matter what her growing up entails.

We have said that God finds children worthy of healing. Going back to the story of the child with meningitis, we can ask how what we have said about God influences our attitudes today. First, we recognize in the story the desperate anxiety of parents who know both that their child is sick and dying and that they must seek healing from those who have the power to save. Consequently it was right to ask whether everything that could be done, was done, in the care and treatment of the child. We learn, too, that no other considerations – being busy, having few resources, being told that there is no point – are more important than making sure that *all* children get an equal and adequate chance to be healed. Moreover, it is also part of God's desire for children that they should get the chance to be nurtured, to flourish and to grow. Consequently, we need to look beyond our own developed nations with their excellent healthcare, to those nations where children have no access to clean water and adequate food or to medicines that would protect them from disease. In this story, Jesus does not stop for *anything* to get to a child apparently beyond all possible help. That is a lesson to us, too.

The healing of the Syro-Phoenician woman's daughter

Just two chapters later, however, another story seems to suggest that other matters may be at play in the matter of access to God's healing power. The story of the Syro-Phoenician woman's daughter is in many ways deeply troubling. Another version of the story is found in Matthew 15.21–28, but we can start with the Markan version:

> From there he set out and went away to the region of Tyre. He entered a house and did not want anyone to know he was there. Yet he could not escape notice, but a woman whose little daughter had an unclean spirit immediately heard about him, and she came and bowed down at his feet. Now the woman was a Gentile, of Syrophoenician origin. She begged him to cast the demon out of her daughter. He said to her, 'Let the children be fed first, for it is not fair to take the children's food and throw it to the dogs.' But she answered him, 'Sir, even the dogs under the table eat the children's crumbs.' Then he said to her, 'For saying that, you may go—the demon has left your daughter.' So she went home, found the child lying on the bed, and the demon gone.
>
> (Mark 7.24–30)

Here we encounter a Jesus who apparently doesn't want to be disturbed, but, like a celebrity who is constantly doorstepped, people find out that he is in the cosmopolitan area of Tyre and hear of his fame as a healer. The pattern is repeated, a woman with a sick child seeks out Jesus and throws herself at his feet. We can only imagine what it took for the woman to get to Jesus when he was trying to stay out of the limelight. Who did she have to bribe, battle, sweet-talk or fight to get through to where he was?[18] In the version in Matthew, we get a flavour of this: she is apparently shouting at Jesus, begging for mercy for her daughter, and profoundly irritating his disciples who want him to get her sent away: 'she keeps shouting after us'. But like the woman with the haemorrhage or the woman seeking Elisha, the mother will stop at nothing to get to the person who can help. Yet after all that, this woman is a Gentile, and Jesus apparently says no.

Why does Jesus say this? His reply is couched in terms of priority service for Jews like himself. Are Jewish people more deserving of healing than others? Matthew's version has Jesus saying that 'I was sent only to the lost sheep of the House of Israel'. Do they have a prior claim on Jesus' ministry as one of their own? Does Jesus only have so much healing power he can dole out at a time (this might be inferred from the story of the woman with a haemorrhage)? Why is Jesus apparently so rude and abrupt – to call the woman a 'dog' was a particular insult, like a slap in the face. One of the questions we have to ask here, quite apart from the fact that we cannot know if these are Jesus' words or not, is, who else was supposed to be listening (or reading) and what else should we remember about what *God* wants?

In this narrative the woman is not going to give up. She argues back, saying that Gentiles may not have a prior claim on Jesus' mission to the Jewish people but that she will take whatever 'crumbs' she can get. The 'dogs' are the lowest of the low, but she will identify with them and turn the image round to one of the household dogs licking up the crumbs which fall (or are fed to them) under the table; let Jesus despise her as an outsider, if only her daughter can be healed. She redraws or reframes the context, as one who is nonetheless part of the household if only 'under the table'. In other words, human issues, politics, priorities, even the indignity which makes some people more 'worthy' than others, can be overturned through faith in God's mercy and justice. Jesus is apparently impressed by this argument, for the woman penetrates to the heart of the matter: God does *not* want children to suffer or die. This is a theological issue, a matter of faith

---

[18] J. Donahue and D. Harrington point out the significance of 'boundary crossings' in this story, *The Gospel of Mark* (Sacra Pagina; Collegeville, MN: The Liturgical Press, 2002), vol. 2, p. 237.

(as we see in the woman with the haemorrhage). Matthew makes this explicit: 'Woman, great is your faith!' She is 'the woman who challenges readers against setting limits to those who would be called sons and daughters of God'.[19]

The most important part of the narrative is its outcome. The child *is* healed. Matthew says 'instantly' but Mark's version is more human and dramatic: the woman is told she doesn't have to try any more, the demon of sickness, whether of physical or mental illness, has gone. But it is not until the woman finds the child on her bed, the demon gone, that the physical reality of that healing is found to match the faith that Jesus will heal her child. It is interesting that here the healing takes place at a distance, just as in Matthew 8.5–13 when the faith of a non-Jew is again the agency which allows healing to take place. The centurion who begs for the life of his servant says, 'Lord, I am not worthy to have you come under my roof; but only speak the word, and my servant will be healed' (Matthew 8.8) and it is reported that Jesus is again amazed by the man's faith: '"Go; let it be done for you according to your faith." And the servant was healed in that hour' (Matthew 8.13). Similarly in John 4.46–54 a Gentile military officer begs Jesus to heal his son who is at the point of death. Jesus says, 'Unless you [plural – Jesus is talking to everybody] see signs and wonders you will not believe'. The officer pleads with Jesus to go to his son, but Jesus tells him to go and promises that his son will live. On the way back home, the man's servants tell him that the child is alive and recovering and that the recovery began at the same time Jesus promised the healing. The result here, John tells us, is that this had an effect on the faith and life of the man and his entire household. For John, the healing at a distance of a child on the point of death is a 'sign' which points to God's desire for the world.

But if healing and faith are intimately related in the way God's presence is recognized in the world, the opposite can also be true:

> On the next day, when they had come down from the mountain, a great crowd met him. Just then a man from the crowd shouted, 'Teacher, I beg you to look at my son; he is my only child. Suddenly a spirit seizes him, and all at once he shrieks. It throws him into

---

[19] Donahue and Harrington, *The Gospel of Mark*, p. 238.

convulsions until he foams at the mouth; it mauls him and will scarcely leave him. I begged your disciples to cast it out, but they could not.' Jesus answered, 'You faithless and perverse generation, how much longer must I be with you and bear with you? Bring your son here.' While he was coming, the demon dashed him to the ground in convulsions. But Jesus rebuked the unclean spirit, healed the boy, and gave him back to his father. And all were astounded at the greatness of God. (Luke 9.37–43)

Here the disciples cannot effect a healing miracle, because their faith that God desires healing for children is simply not strong enough. The epileptic child seems beyond help. Yet Jesus can restore the child to his father. When someone is terribly ill or has been badly hurt in an accident, the injuries or symptoms can frighten us, so that we lose the ability to imagine how they can get well. Yet when the disease or injuries are treated and healing takes place we may look back and realize how we did not at first believe that the person could get better. When the disciples see the child in convulsions they lose the ability to imagine the child as God sees him; they see only the here and now. What Jesus does is to reframe the issue. He looks beyond the immediate into the kingdom reality which mirrors God's desire and gives *that* child to his father. That is the place we inhabit by faith and it is this which the disciples have forgotten. David Ford, talking about people with disabilities at L'Arche, calls it 'waiting for the beauty'.[20]

Feeding and healing

Another significant matter in the stories of Jairus' daughter and the Syro-Phoenician woman is the link between feeding and healing. Jesus tells the girl's parents that the child must be fed; the dispensation of healing to the Syro-Phoenician woman's daughter is carried out in terms of feeding crumbs. We see this reflected in some Eucharistic liturgies where these stories are remembered in prayers before communion. So we should also remember that often at the heart of our worship is a plea for healing, but also that it links to a mother's pleas for her child.

---

[20] D. Ford, *The Shape of Living* (London: HarperCollins, 1997), p. 101.

What does all this tell us? First, that God finds all people, no matter how underprivileged or badly viewed by other human beings, worthy of healing. That especially includes children. No matter how helpless, vulnerable or ruined by disease, God's desire is that children should be made whole and allowed to flourish. But God's agency is not *just* healing. These narratives also show that God finds the lowest of the low, irrespective of birth, race, region or sex, worthy of recognition, worthy of love, worthy of health, and so God shows other people just how wrong it is to judge one human life against another, or to privilege one person's religion, status or adulthood over others'. When these healings glorify God it is not just that a child recovers health and wellbeing, but that the child represents something about God's justice too. The healed child is a 'sign' of God's justice becoming manifest in the world around us.

Second, the person who pleads for the lives of the suffering is important. The centurion tells Jesus that his servant is 'in terrible distress' (Matthew 8.6). While his servant represents an economic and social asset to him, it is pain that he reports. Similarly the parents of the suffering children bring that suffering before Jesus and speak on behalf of that pain. Speaking on behalf of the suffering and in the desire that their pain should be overcome is important. The people whom Jesus helps have the ability to bring the absent child powerfully before him and to make that child present. It is perhaps this making present of the suffering child that creates the space for Jesus to bring healing into the child's life; for the petitioners are suffering too and their worry and fear is also healed. The hope that they carry back with them translates into joy, relief, and a stronger spirituality and faith. The healing of a child affects the spiritual health of the whole family.

Third, persistence in faith matters too. The Gentile woman may only be offered crumbs but her belief in the reality of those crumbs in her daughter's life is just as strong as the full 'meal'. The clear-eyed recognition of who Jesus is and that he only needs to speak a word or that a person need only touch him, teaches us something about faith. It is not about getting hold of Jesus' attention and making him 'perform' but about how his presence sharpens and directs the understanding that God does not want children to die, but to be healed, to be made whole.

Finally, these narratives offer us a very simple truth. How do we know that God finds children worthy of healing? Because these children *are* healed. The dead child may be buried, lost and forgotten, but the healed child carries in his body every day the reality that God has a desire and purpose for his life which adults cannot and should not deny.

How does this help us understand the world we live in? We can be sure that the sickness and death of children is not God's will. The lamentation heard in Ramah for the death of children is a real cry of protest to God which is heard by God. We also learn that the suffering and fear of parents merits God's compassion and mercy, no matter what human obstacles seem to stand in the way. And further we learn that faith has a part in creating a healing relationship between God and the child. What God wills for each child is a healthy environment in which that child will be able to flourish and grow.

If we compare that to the world we know, then we can see that reality is very different. We have already seen that children do suffer and die in terrible circumstances, even in our own society. Some cases of child suffering and death become notorious, such as the deaths of Baby Peter and Victoria Climbié as we saw in Chapter 2. Yet we may say that the very outrage and distress we feel when such cases are made known through the media makes us one with the parents who fought their way through the crowds to ask Jesus for help. The difference is that we do not often see the relationship between healing and justice – we want retribution and punishment for those who put children beyond help.

Some questions for reflection
- What are your own experiences of looking after sick children?
- How can we see recovery from sickness as a sign of God's kingdom?
- Why do you think Jesus said 'no' to the Syro-Phoenician woman?
- What more do we need to do to make sure children are not neglected, cruelly treated or abused?

Activity
Find out about the work of charities which help children who are ill or dying. What *one* thing might you be able to do to support or aid such work?

5

God finds children worthy of blessing

'Grace . . .'

People were bringing little children to him in order that he might touch them; and the disciples spoke sternly to them. But when Jesus saw this, he was indignant and said to them, 'Let the little children come to me; do not stop them; for it is to such as these that the kingdom of God belongs. Truly I tell you, whoever does not receive the kingdom of God as a little child will never enter it.' And he took them up in his arms, laid his hands on them, and blessed them.

(Mark 10.13–16)

Then little children were being brought to him in order that he might lay his hands on them and pray. The disciples spoke sternly to those who brought them; but Jesus said, 'Let the little children come to me, and do not stop them; for it is to such as these that the kingdom of heaven belongs.' And he laid his hands on them and went on his way.

(Matthew 19.13–15)

In thinking about these famous passages from the Gospels, I casually Googled 'let the little children come to me' and selected 'images'. What immediately came up on my screen was a succession of sentimental and idealized images. Jesus, sitting in a beautiful pastoral landscape, cuddles a succession of young children who gaze up at him adoringly, with the occasional baby lamb thrown in. There is no sign of the disciples, or of the children's mothers. Jesus smiles beatifically, sometimes with a halo added for good measure. These pictures radiate comfort, sweetness, joy.

These kinds of images are very different from earlier treatments in art. One artist who painted the subject many times for different patrons was Lucas Cranach the Elder (1472–1553) and the subject was also treated by his son Lucas Cranach the Younger (1515–1586). In these paintings, the disciples are relegated, frowning, to the edges of the paintings, while many women are admitted to the centre of the painting with Jesus. Jesus ends up surrounded by naked babies and typically lays one hand on a child held out to him by the mother, while holding another in his other arm. Cranach depicts mothers suckling their children, pulling recalcitrant infants along into Jesus' orbit. In one painting, a child brings her doll along as well; in another a child tries not to get squashed in the press of people.[1] Both Cranachs dress the women in the garb of their own time, and paint from their own observations of family life. Yet the subject is still idealized. Although now we have more of the participants, more observed behaviour of the disciples as henchmen and women trying to cope with children, in the centre Jesus is still radiating unearthly calm, dispensing divine grace, while disappearing into the sea of babies.

Jesus as rejected child

But to my mind this leaves a very awkward question about Jesus himself in this passage. We have mostly read it the way we want to read it, with the focus on the children, who get to be patted on the head or cuddled by Jesus – the way we often treat children in church in fact when they are allowed to show us their drawings and go back to their seats with some half-hearted applause. This leaves a serious question which needs to be answered: *why was Jesus so angry?* The word translated 'indignant' does not really give the force of Jesus' reaction. He is furious, seething. But why would Jesus get so worked up about this particular occasion?

I think we have to reach further back into the heart of the Gospels and ask how Jesus creates family. He certainly had a family: Mary, his mother, is present in various scenarios within the Gospels. Mark 6.3 says 'Is this not the carpenter, the son of Mary and brother of James and Joses and Judas and Simon, and are not his sisters here with us?'[2] There has been much speculation about the precise relationship of Jesus to these brothers and sisters, with some suggesting that they were further children of Joseph and Mary. Others have

---

[1] See, for example, *Christ Blessing the Children*, c. 1535–40, Städel Museum, Frankfurt; Lucas Cranach the Younger and Workshop, *Christ Blessing the Children*, 1515–86, Metropolitan Museum, New York.

[2] Mark 6.3; Matthew 13.55; John 7.3; Acts 1.14; 1 Corinthians 9.5.

thought that because Joseph disappears from mention, he might have been an older widowed man with existing children who then formed part of Jesus' family. The apocryphal gospels which stress the virginity of Mary certainly like to portray Joseph as an old man who had adopted Mary and Jesus into his larger family. Or is it possible that the 'brothers and sisters' were cousins or other relatives who belonged to Jesus' kinship network? In Josephus, there is an external corroboration of Jesus and James being brothers, so it is very likely that there was a close connection between them.[3] Whatever the case, Mark 6.1–6 gives us a strong hint that the relationship between Jesus and his family and community was not an easy one. Jesus goes back to his home town and teaches in the synagogue, but all the people there, who know him, take 'offence' at him. Jesus says that 'Prophets are not without honour, except in their home town, and among their own kin, and in their own house' and the writer of Mark reports that he was not able to do much except heal a few people. In Luke 4, the people of Nazareth are 'filled with rage' by his teaching and try to 'hurl him off the cliff' (vv. 28, 29).

What must all that have been like for Jesus' family? If he was a half-brother to other older children, they might well have resented this younger child, a cuckoo in the nest, especially if he was particularly favoured by their father and stepmother. In Luke 2 we're told about the anxious search for Jesus, left behind in Jerusalem. How might the other family children have reacted to Jesus as he grew up? Did they think he was strange, crazy, megalomaniac, attention-seeking, a pain in the neck? Is he like Joseph, he of the coat of many colours, resented by his brothers and thrown into a pit (Genesis 37.3–4, 23–24)? We get a picture of this in Mark 3.19–20 when we are told that 'he went home; and the crowd came together again, so that they could not even eat. When his family heard it, they went out to restrain him, for people were saying, "He has gone out of his mind".' Reidar Aasgaard brings home to us the central role of honour and shame in families of this time. Your name, your status, how you dressed and your profession made an important difference to how you were regarded in the community: 'to be blamed publicly meant social degradation, loss of face, and had to be met by counterattack; one's honour had to be

---

[3] Josephus, *Antiquities of the Jews*, 20.9.1.

retrieved, by retaliation, aggressiveness, and display of authority and boldness'.[4] Jesus' behaviour must have seriously compromised the family's honour. Whatever he meant to them, it is likely that there were some serious rows about what he was doing and how he behaved. Perhaps the rift was even worse than this. Matthew 12.46–50 tells us that Jesus' mother and brothers came to where he was speaking and waited outside wanting to talk to him. When Jesus was told about this, he is reported to have said 'Who is my mother, and who are my brothers?' and pointed to his disciples, including in the answer to his question, 'whoever does the will of my Father'. We can only speculate, but perhaps Jesus was completely run out of town and rejected even by his own family. The passage in Mark about the unhonoured prophet is followed by the instruction to the disciples to shake the dust off their feet at households which will not welcome them (Mark 6.10–11).

Rejection must have been a powerful experience in his ministry, but we tend to focus on the miracles and sayings which take place among adoring crowds, not the times when Jesus and his disciples were sent packing. Yet Jesus speaks powerfully of rejected and abandoned people, such as the victim in the parable of the Good Samaritan, and he goes out of his way to help those who have been abandoned, such as the Gerasene demoniac. Further, Jesus does not seem to have gone home again after these reported notices to cease and desist. Jesus is reported as saying in Luke 9.58 that 'Foxes have holes, and birds of the air have their nests; but the Son of Man has nowhere to lay his head' and immediately following this, in reply to would-be followers who ask first to say goodbye to their families or to organize a funeral for a family member, they are told not to bother. 'Let the dead bury their own dead' seems particularly bitter, and Jesus tells them that looking back is no good if you want to be fit for the kingdom of God.

So if Jesus felt like a rejected child, rebuked by his own family, dragged off in a cloud of shame for pursuing his ministry, we can begin to see where the anger of Mark 10.13–16 comes from, and how the disciples, shouting at the mothers with children and pushing them away, would trigger it. What is also significant is that Jesus,

---

[4] R. Aasgaard, *My Beloved Brothers and Sisters: Christian Siblingship in Paul* (London: T&T Clark, 2004), pp. 51–2.

unmarried, and apparently without other family obligations, goes about creating new families. The tribal genealogical family, like the one set out at the beginning of Matthew's Gospel for Jesus himself, the pattern of family descent represented by all those 'begats' in the Hebrew Scriptures, is interrupted by Jesus when he creates different and other kinship networks based on spiritual relationships who draw their closeness and companionship from the common parenthood of the Father. He calls the disciples to become his brothers; he forms important friendships with other families like that of Mary, Martha and Lazarus. And we see him befriending other friendless and rejected people: Mary Magdalene and Zacchaeus, for example. Rejection and betrayal are powerful themes in the Gospels, and Jesus continually points to God as the Father who never gives up on the rejected child, no matter how far away he is or what he might have done.

For me, this idea of Jesus as the rejected child who has shamed the family gives the parable of the Prodigal Son a particular poignancy, especially the furious annoyance of the 'good' brother who has stayed at home and not shamed the family honour by demanding his inheritance before the father is dead. Similarly, the parable of the wedding feast in which all the invited people are shut out and the people 'both good and bad' without invitations are let in, may also derive its vividness from Jesus' personal experience (Matthew 22.1–14). But if God is the loving Father who never rejects his child, there is yet for Jesus the inability of his disciple 'family' to keep up with him in his suffering in the Garden of Gethsemane and the cry of abandonment from the cross. Yet John's Gospel tells us that Jesus continued to create family even at his crucifixion, giving his mother into the care of 'the disciple whom he loved . . . "Woman, here is your son"' (John 19.26).

If Jesus creates new theological notions of family, then how are people expected to shift their thinking, action and experience into this new mode of being? After all, the people around Jesus were brought up with powerful notions of lineage and relationship. We can see this in the glimpses of the long history of hatred between Jews and Samaritans which most of Jesus' contemporaries would have taken as absolute, consolidated by history. Yet Jesus overturns even this historic rift in his parable of the Good Samaritan and his conversation with the woman at the well. People hearing about this must have struggled with the weight of ancestral prejudice in order to get their heads round what Jesus was saying. However, in terms of reframing how families work in God's kingdom, and finding out what God wants for people within the new order, I suggest that Jesus gives us his vision in the conversation with Nicodemus. Jesus says,

> 'Very truly, I tell you, no one can see the kingdom of God without being born from above.' Nicodemus said to him, 'How can anyone be born after having grown old? Can one enter a second time into the mother's womb and be born?'   (John 3.3–4)

This theological conversation uses the language of (re)birth as a reframing of a person's life and purpose with reference to God. Such a reframing results in a spiritual orientation, through the Spirit, that now surrounds the believer as a newborn person within a loving family, of whom the Abba is God. To find oneself newly born in such a family is to discover a spirituality that is life-affirming, not life-denying, as Jesus goes on to explain (John 3.16–21).

I suggest, then, that it is Jesus' own experience of rejection, of difficult family encounters, and his profound need to create family and loving relationships that is at the back of his explosion at the disciples. God finds children worthy of blessing, of being given time, acceptance and privilege. Yet in the human world, some adults decide who can and cannot have access to Jesus, pushing other people to the bottom of the pile, protecting his honour and status and deeming him too important to deal with mere children. I see this as opening Jesus' own personal wounds; his theological conviction about the love of the Father prompts him to use the event to make a powerful statement about a world where God's purposes will be paramount.

So what Jesus does next shocks the disciples – he insists that those with the least case for his attention get all of it. He demands that children should be allowed to come to him and he physically embraces them. When the translation says that he blesses them, it is perhaps difficult for us to get the picture. The sense of the Greek *kateulogei* is that Jesus repeatedly blesses them 'again and again' – so that every-one looking on could not help but understand that the Teacher was giving children his attention, welcome and love. Every child is welcomed and proclaimed to be good in God's sight. God finds in children a community of grace. This means that: the children encounter Jesus' physical reality; the children encounter Jesus's loving embrace; the children are blessed by Jesus repeatedly; there is powerful affirmation in the life of the child; and the child is privileged in front of all the adults. All of these things have both social and theological importance.

So what exactly *is* blessing?

Perhaps, then, Jesus saw himself in the rejected children. He shouts at the disciples (who were perhaps shocked and confused at his reaction) and demands that the children be allowed to approach him. Then he blesses them. But what does this mean and why is this action by Jesus so important?

The Hebrew tradition understood something very fundamental about the act of blessing, which was both sign and full of meaning and purpose. The famous Aaronic blessing occurs in Numbers 6.22–26. God tells Moses that Aaron's blessing will say: 'May the Lord bless you and guard you. May the Lord light up His face to you and grant grace to you; May the Lord lift up His face to you and give you peace.'[5] Blessing them comes with the desire and promise to protect the recipient. The lighting of the face signifies affection and favour, and what flows from the one who blesses to the one who is blessed is grace and peace. As Ephraim Radner says, 'Blessing is life created by and from God, a life that gives life and extends life . . . [it] does stress something central from the Old Testament's understanding of blessing: the sense, as God creates, that "it is good." To bless something, in the New Testament, is to disclose its goodness as from God, as from God's creative hand for God's life-giving purpose.'[6]

So the act of blessing goes back to the fact that God finds the creation to be good, and names the essential goodness of things, and such blessing contains powerful affirmations and love. The opposite of blessing is cursing, which is to name the evil which exists in the world. So God curses the serpent after the Fall. We also see Jesus bestowing both blessing and cursing as ritual acts which name what is good and what is evil before God. Such acts also require an

---

[5] Alter, *The Five Books of Moses*, p. 714. The liturgical form of this blessing is typically 'The Lord bless you and keep you; the Lord make his face to shine upon you, and be gracious to you; the Lord lift up his countenance upon you, and give you peace'.

[6] E. Radner, 'Blessing: A Scriptural and Theological Reflection', a paper presented to the clergy conference of the Diocese of Ontario on 16 June 2009 online at <http://fulcrum-anglican.org.uk/page.cfm?ID=436>.

authority – to be able to name what is good in the creation and what is not. The bestowing of blessing is a serious business, since it emulates the primordial acts of God. Blessing is also not about external attributes, like a getting a gold star for a particularly good piece of homework; it is about naming the essentials of things.

Blessing is also a dynamic process which not only acts as a sign to those who witness it, but also makes a space for the presence of God, for God to be operative. So we find Jesus saying a blessing over the bread at the Last Supper. To pronounce a blessing describes the place where God's grace is to be found, opening a holy space where transformation can take place. When we say that children are worthy of blessing, then we are saying something very serious about the relationship between God and children, something which Jesus made manifest when he demanded that the disciples allow the children to come to him and blessed them.

So every child who is excluded from school, every 'difficult' child, every child who goes off the rails, every adolescent stomping off in a huff, every child who brings 'shame' on the family, all these are pronounced 'good' by Jesus in the act of blessing. There is no child anywhere who deserves less than the unconditional love of God, and if we want to share God's kingdom then we too must find ways to allow such children to come to us and be blessed and to discern where children can find and know themselves blessed.

How might that happen? Two stories come to mind. In James Herriot's books about his life as a rural vet he tells the story of a local bad boy, ten-year-old Wesley Binks. Today, he would probably end up with an ASBO, but in those days the boy was just constantly shouted at and told off for pilfering, vandalism and generally annoying the people of the town. Except one day the child turned up at the vet's surgery with a dog suffering from distemper. Herriot thought the case was probably hopeless but he agreed to try and save the animal. When he visited the home, he discovered indifferent parents who cared neither about the boy nor his suffering pet. Both of them were suffering together. Yet when Herriot began to treat the animal, he enlisted the boy's help and at once a transformation took place. The boy began to run errands to earn pennies for the dog's treatment; he spent hours looking after the dog. He became polite, hard-working and applied all his considerable energy to the project of saving the dog.

But the dog died. And shortly afterwards, the boy was back to his old ways of stealing and vandalism. The townspeople wrote him off as a 'bad 'un' who would never amount to anything', but Herriot remarks in the book that he felt he had looked through a window into the boy's soul and seen the person he really was, capable of such immense love. No one had seen it, except the one person the boy had turned to for help. And the window was only open for a short time, and then it closed.[7]

I find that story instructive. In a world which didn't care about him, the child's spirituality had to find expression. He found the love and companionship God wants for all children in the only being willing to give it to him: his dog. And that love and caring transformed his dealings with the rest of the world. In the small world of indifference and uncaring that was the child's existence, we can imagine that every time the dog wagged its tail or licked his hands, the child felt blessed. It was the one thing that offered him the essential goodness and rightness of God's creation. It could have been the making of him, but when the dog died, the child's blessing disappeared too.

A few years ago a family moved into the area where I lived. They had a young son and his mother was always coming round to see me in despair. Jamie was rude, aggressive and refused to go to school. He kicked anyone who came near him. I would say things like 'Hello Jamie, how are you?' and he would reply 'I HATE YOU! AND I HATE YOUR CAR!' Jamie's parents tried buying him toys (smashed and broken) and pets (kicked and screamed at), but nothing seemed to distract Jamie from his constant fight with the world. Although several years younger than my own two children he hung around after them, plaintively asking to play with them, but when they invited him round to play he didn't seem to know how to and ended up screaming at them before storming off in tears and rage. Doctors offered different opinions about whether he was autistic or not (undecided), schoolteachers despaired about whether he would ever get to stay in school (doubtful), social workers visited to see what his home life was like (no problems), his parents argued about whether it was a good idea to have any more children. Jamie shouted and ran from all of them.

One day, I was putting stuff in the back of my car when Jamie turned up and demanded to know what I was doing. I told him we were going

---

[7] J. Herriot, *Vets Might Fly* (London: Pan, 2006 [1976]), ch. 5, pp. 48–59.

on holiday. 'WHAT ARE YOU GOING TO GET ME?' he screamed. His mother hurried over, apologizing and telling him he shouldn't be asking me for things. 'SHUT UP!' he roared in her face and then to me, 'I WANT A TRACTOR!' When I returned, I gave him a toy tractor I'd bought him, much to his mother's scarlet-faced embarrassment. But, like the dog in the Herriot story, Jamie seemed to be transformed by the tractor. He took it everywhere and played with it constantly, in the rain, in the dark, but always outside. Then he began to tell my children stories about it: 'MY TRACTOR IS IN THE FIELD!' he yelled over the fence at them. 'GREAT!' they shouted back.

One day Jamie's mother came round to tell me they were moving – to a small farm a few miles away. Jamie's tractor-life had so invaded theirs that they began to wonder whether that would in fact help him to settle down and find some peace. They said that when they had gone to look at the broken-down farm, a smallholding that had belonged to an elderly widow, and requiring so much work, and so much effort, they had been amazed by the way Jamie had reacted to the isolated fields and the lack of other houses and car noise. It was as if he had 'really found himself', his mother told me. One day about a year later I was driving my younger son to visit one of his friends in a village about ten miles away. As I drove along the winding country road I passed by the little farm. In the field at the edge of the road I suddenly saw Jamie. He was riding on a tractor-mower with his dad, cutting the grass, standing between his dad's legs with his arms in the air, his face turned to the sky, beaming. He looked blessed.

These stories remind me that the way children find blessing is not only different from child to child but may seem to us trivial or far from the things we think are important. These instances of blessing, the boy's dog, and Jamie's outdoor life on the farm, become evident because they shine out from the difficulty and darkness of the rest of these children's lives. For some children, who are not 'difficult', identifying the things which make them feel blessed may be even harder to identify.

But here's a different story. When I was 12 I made friends with a girl called Jane. Jane went to another school, but we were both learning German. She was extremely clever – and extremely good at German. We used to meet at the bus station after school. I liked her. She was funny and made me laugh. We joked about friends and teachers. We compared German homework answers. We made up impromptu sketches in which all the characters spoke a terrible mix of German and English. She was always cheerful. But then, I stopped seeing Jane. I wondered what had happened to her. I missed her and her anarchic sense of humour. A few weeks later I read a story in the local paper which carried a report about her. Jane was dead. She had killed herself. She was 12 years old.

Jane's story also makes us aware that children can feel excluded, shunned or cursed. In Herriot's example, the indifference and lack of love in the boy's family made him feel cursed and he acted out that curse on other people. In Jamie's life, a fear of being indoors and the proximity of other people, the pressure to conform to what others expected of him, also cursed his life. Sadly we hear of many children who are cursed by their lives: children who are bullied, children who are abused, children who are neglected or hurt or ignored. We find them as runaways, sleeping on the streets and vulnerable to those who prey on them; we find them as suicides. Yet in the case of Jane, no matter how many times I went over my relationship with her in my mind, I could not detect one trace of whatever happened in her life to make her end it. It remains for me an extraordinary mystery for which I retain a powerful feeling of guilt and emptiness. Was I not friend enough for her to confide in me; were the things that might have happened to her too terrible to articulate; did I contribute to her feelings of low-esteem or inadequacy or depression; did I simply feed off her cheerfulness and wit without care for anything else she might feel, or did I simply not penetrate enough into her world to make a difference to the place she was going? Or was I simply being arrogant in assuming that I had any impact in her life at all and whatever was going on in her life was beyond the reach of a childhood friendship? Sometimes it is a mystery why some people feel that they have no blessings left to count.

Parenthood and blessing

In Matthew 7.9–11 Jesus says:

> 'Is there anyone among you who, if your child asks for bread, will give a stone? Or if the child asks for a fish, will give a snake? If you then, who are evil, know how to give good gifts to your children, how much more will your Father in heaven give good things to those who ask him?'

We might link this to sayings where Jesus is trying to make people see the relationship between human beings and God. God is Abba, whose relationship with human beings is as intimate as parent and child. God knows what we need and responds to our needs; God gives us what is good for us. God's only desire is to bless us and for us to know that we are blessed. What true parent gives a child a stone when he asks for bread, a snake when he asks for a fish? God knows what we need, what makes us aware of the essential goodness at the heart of things so that we feel blessed. And God's over-abundance of gift is made manifest in the miracle of the loaves and fishes. This tells us that the act of blessing is life-extending; blessing creates better social conditions; blessing opens up a burgeoning and flourishing spiritual life; blessing allows people to see the essential goodness of creation and to know that God is at the heart of it.

Children need a space in which they can explore the encounter with the Abba who is God. But that space is so difficult to find. Too often, there are adults in the way, crowding out the space and hiding God from view. Children might obtain glimpses of God perhaps through the legs of the adults, but for them to have a complete opportunity depends on the adults realizing that, often, *they are in the way*.

For example, I recently went to my brother-in-law's birthday party with my husband and sons. My brother-in-law has twin two-year-old boys. There were about eight children of various ages at the party playing with each other and the family dog. Various adults I noticed were playing on and off with the twins, but in particular ways. One thing I noticed is that they talked a lot, telling the children what to do (and what not to do), but this meant that although they gave the children a lot of attention, they didn't really notice what the children got out of it. One adult very painstakingly helped the children make a sandcastle and then was clearly upset when, having turned it out, they gaily smashed it to pieces. Similarly, another adult was kindly helping one of the twins to the top of the playslide but then almost pushing him down the slide itself. The adult had assumed that the point of climbing the slide was to get the excitement of going down it, but as far as I could see the excitement for the child *was just to get to the top of the slide*, to have a different vantage point, to see the garden from a whole new angle. But he had hardly had a chance to look around and glory in the view, when he was whizzing down to the bottom and had to start again.

But later, I watched my son Jonathan play football with one of the twins, Matthew. He didn't say anything to the child at all, but he made the ball work so that it landed exactly where the twin could kick it or handle it; he didn't try to bamboozle him with his superior skills, just kept giving the ball back in exactly the place the child wanted. The twin, who had been frowning earlier as the ball kept getting away or was frustrated as the adults whipped it past him, played for about 15 minutes with a smile of pure delight on his face. Eventually, he was sated with the game and asked Jonathan to sit down. Matthew climbed on his lap with the ball and Jonathan put his arms round him. You do not give children stones when they ask for bread. But knowing exactly what they want and need and being able to give it to them is a rare gift, a blessing.

It seems to me that this simple communion between adults and children is just such a gift. It suggests that we ought to pay more attention to the signals children send us about what they want and need and to hold back from our more obvious assumptions about what they need. That's not an easy thing to do, often, because we are conditioned to care. I remember fighting with one of my children who wanted to go out and play when it was snowing. I was bundling him into a warm coat, a scarf, wellies, a hat, gloves, the lot. No sooner had I got a glove or a welly on, than they came straight off again. Eventually, after about 15 minutes of wailing and frustration, my friend who was watching all this observed that Philip wanted to go out and *feel* the snow. He wanted to get cold and wet and frozen and stuff the flakes into his mouth and eyes. It sometimes takes an outsider's eye to see how all our caring gets in the way of what the child really needs and to persuade the parent that where he or she needs to be is on the other side, with a warm towel and a hot drink.

The obstacles between children and God

To return to the passages about Jesus and the children, we need to dig deeper into what seems to be taking place. First, there is the familiar sight of the disciples trying to shield Jesus from the crowd and making decisions about who does and who does not get access to the Teacher. As we saw in Chapter 3, like a modern celebrity, Jesus is being mobbed by people who, instead of wanting an autograph, want him to notice them and respond to their petitions. We are told that people are bringing their children to him, perhaps for healing, perhaps for his attention, but the disciples, like publicists and PR managers, decide that they must be turned away.

In Jesus' time this made sense. Women and children were integral parts of Jewish society but not the most important members. In terms of a pecking order they were non-persons, people who would be at the bottom of the heap. Yet we know from the Gospels that Jesus constantly astonished his disciples by going out of his way to respond to such people: women, foreigners, the sick, the despised and the mad.

A child in the midst

At that time the disciples came to Jesus and asked, 'Who is the greatest in the kingdom of heaven?' He called a child, whom he put among them, and said, 'Truly I tell you, unless you change and become like children, you will never enter the kingdom of heaven. Whoever becomes humble like this child is the greatest in the kingdom of heaven. Whoever welcomes one such child in my name welcomes me.

'If any of you put a stumbling-block before one of these little ones who believe in me, it would be better for you if a great millstone were fastened around your neck and you were drowned in the depth of the sea. Woe to the world because of stumbling-blocks! Occasions for stumbling are bound to come, but woe to the one by whom the stumbling-block comes!'   (Matthew 18.1–7)

The blessing of the children can be compared with these passages in which Jesus privileges a child to make a point. In Mark 9.35–37, 42 and in Matthew, quoted above, the disciples are arguing about who is the greatest among them. Jesus stops the argument by turning the language on its head by a visual demonstration. Calling a child, he places the child among the quarrelling disciples and says that the answer to their dispute lies in their noticing and understanding the essential qualities of being a child. They need to change and to be like the child, who knows from her daily existence that she is not great and not considered great. 'Children's vulnerability and powerlessness seem to lie at the heart of Jesus' extension of the reign of God to them.'[8]

---

[8] J. Gundry-Volf, 'The Least and the Greatest: Children in the New Testament', in M. Bunge (ed.), *The Child in Christian Thought* (Grand Rapids, MI: Eerdmans, 2001), p. 38.

Appearance, ambition and self-regard are of no use to her and so she is more prepared for a meaningful kingdom relationship with God than the disciples are. Again we glimpse Jesus' passion about the acceptance and notice due to the child in God's family. Whoever welcomes the child welcomes Jesus and whoever hurts, ignores or prevents children from having access to the loving Father God will feel the full force of the divine passion that finds children worthy of blessing. Jesus' message is stark, a curse: 'It would be better for you if a great millstone were hung around your neck and you were thrown into the sea' (Mark 9.42). There is a mirroring of actions. If a child is pushed away from God then the effect on your own relationship with God is to put this vast distance between you and the Father, as you disappear, dragged down into the depths away from the light. Children, however, are already close to God's heart: 'in heaven their angels continually see the face of my Father in heaven' (Matthew 18.10). Jesus combines the language of closeness and distance with the way the disciples behave both among themselves and towards children. He also seems to have cared about the way children believed in and responded to him. In the blessing of the children, the visual message would have been that the adults looking on would have seen the children between themselves and Jesus. The children would have had the longed-for closeness. In the version in Luke, you could not get to Jesus without acknowledging the presence of the child.

> An argument arose among them as to which one of them was the greatest. But Jesus, aware of their inner thoughts, took a little child and put it by his side, and said to them, 'Whoever welcomes this child in my name welcomes me, and whoever welcomes me welcomes the one who sent me; for the least among all of you is the greatest.'
>
> (Luke 9.46–48)

Here the theological point is especially clear: every person who hopes for heaven must be(come) like a child.

This reminds me of a strange little vignette in Matthew 11.16–17. Jesus says:

> 'But to what will I compare this generation? It is like children sitting in the market-places and calling to one another, "We played the flute for you, and you did not dance; we wailed, and you did not mourn."'

If we leave the simile aside initially, we see that Jesus notices and brings to adult attention the way that children play together. Perhaps he remembers playing the same games himself. The children enact what the adults do, playing at pretend weddings – playing the flute and dancing, or a funeral game – wailing and mourning. The children call to their friends to join in, the play, the game, is in full flow, but there are some who won't heed the call. If there are some who won't play, won't experience how life and death works in human society, then they will not have gone through the spiritual exploration and testing necessary to understand the message which John the Baptist and Jesus bring. It is very interesting that Jesus uses children's play as a test of spiritual openness, and fits with his desire to use children as illustrations of how God's kingdom works and his wish to bless them. 'Jesus . . . taught the arrival of a social world in part defined by and organized around children.'[9] Similarly, after the event when Jesus falls into a fury and smashes the tables of the moneychangers in the Temple, we are told that the chief priests and scribes are angry about the children praising and calling out to Jesus, but Jesus turns their words back on them by quoting Scripture suggesting that it is the children whose spiritual sight is most clear and whose cries are truth (Psalm 8.2; Matthew 21.16).

I was thinking about this recently when I was again playing with my twin nephews at their house. They had a big tub of building blocks and I spent the afternoon sitting on the floor building roads (straight and angled), towers, castles and entire churches (converted with narthex and disabled access via various ingenious ramp systems). All my buildings were cheerfully destroyed as soon as completed, and the empty tub placed on my head as a hat. It occurred to me though that the children's enjoyment in the games we played was in the *making*. They enjoyed watching and helping me build something out of the blocks and as soon as that was done, there was a sheer pleasure in starting all over again to make something new. It was only the adults who regretted the work that had been put in, and the loss of the achievement, the finished object. For the children, play was endless possibility, the joy of creation, the very unknowing of what might emerge from the play next. If Jesus' words about children's play mean something in the context of spiritual learning and the knowledge that we are blessed,

---

[9] Gundry-Volf, 'The Least and the Greatest', p. 60.

it is that we should understand what play means, the unfolding of a continuous and unexpected and delightful narrative of being and making that does not become a static monument but a permanent dance of delight. It is when we remember how to do this that we become receptive to change, to being remoulded by God into beings fit for God's reconciled and redeemed world.

Privileging children

To continue this theme, another way to get at the depths of the passages in which Jesus blesses children is to try and imagine what it was like for those children, having been denied and rejected by Jesus' own friends, to find themselves invited to meet him and be blessed by him. We have, I suspect, a faint echo in the commercialized wrappings of the Santa grotto, when as parents we pay ridiculous prices for our children to go in to meet a person in a costume who talks with them about what they want for Christmas and perhaps (if they're lucky) gives them a small gift. The essence of such a ritual for the child, though, is the few seconds of privilege – what *you* want; a chance to share hopes and dreams. Of course, a lot of this is lost in the bargain about whether the child has been 'good' and in the sense of reward as material things, but somewhere in all of it is a sense of wonder at meeting someone completely rare who will (supposedly) see into your soul and hear your heart's desire. Perhaps it is some inkling of the blessing of the children that creates those long queues at Christmas.

The problem we have is that we don't look at it from the child's point of view or imagine what such a moment might do for a child's spirituality. We tend to think of such events in patronizing terms, patting children on the head and indulging them, rather than really engaging with the essence of who they are. The nearest way I have been able to imagine it comes from rather a strange source:

When my children were primary school age we went to San Diego in California. One of the things my sons most remember was going to a restaurant downtown. The reason we chose this particular restaurant was because it was supposed to be a kid's dream place to eat. The food came in buckets and you had to eat messily with your fingers with a paper bib round your neck, and the waiters all made a huge fuss of the children and were rude to the adults. Our children loved it when they were served first and we were made to wait, and when they asked for more drink or straws, they were brought lots of drinks and whole packets of straws, while we were told to get to the back of the line and the waiters would think about bringing us a drink, *if* we behaved ourselves. The waiters criticized the adults' food choices, dress, manners and told us all off, while praising the children and inviting them to talk about themselves. They were brought crayons, balloons and free extras and when we complained we were told we wouldn't be getting ice cream for being whiners. I still remember Philip's eyes shining with a mixture of glee and incredulity as his plate was filled to over-flowing with ice cream while I had a tiny blob on mine.

The last shall be first . . . the restaurant really brought home to me what that might mean, not as a pious phrase but in reality. My children did not dream of being first to be served, of being allowed to make decisions, of being praised and showered with attention – that's not what their experience of restaurants was like. Yet on this occasion they were first at the feast, offered the best of everything; when they asked for anything, a surfeit appeared – a picture Jesus offers of life in God's kingdom, where the least in our world experience firsthand the Father's overflowing love.

So the blessing of children offers privileging, visibility, an order in the creation, a vision of God's heavenly world and intention, a sign, a message, and a profound affirmation of the child *as a* child.

The Church as God's young family

The first time I ever visited Spain my two children were very young and quickly got bored with sightseeing. They wanted fun (and paella). I remember very clearly taking them to a children's playground and letting them play on the swings in the sunshine. At first the play-ground was deserted, but after a few minutes a group of local children entered. They played by themselves for a few minutes, and then went over to my children and asked them a question. My children didn't understand. There was a few seconds of confusion, but then everyone smiled at one another, and by gestures and laughing and clowning around after two more minutes everyone was playing together. All the children played for the next hour seamlessly, understanding one another, getting off the swings and pushing each other by turns;

chasing and being chased, helping the smallest get up the slide and giving her a hug when she fell off the rubber tyre. Small clashes over what was going to happen next disappeared into jokes and exaggerated acting. Play erased the language barrier and created instant bonds of generosity. When we left, my children brought me over to their new friends and 'interpreted' for me, introducing them and telling me all about them, although no actual information could have been exchanged in words. We all shook hands. Then the others left saying 'See you tomorrow' in Spanish. 'OK,' my children replied.

In her work on children's spirituality Rebecca Nye has directed attention to the fact that spirituality is constituted by so much more than words. Indeed she identifies spirituality with 'space', 'process', 'imagination', 'relationship', 'intimacy' and 'trust'.[10] Consequently, we can argue that spiritual processes are at work in the business of finding a way to be and to play together and this is what I saw in evidence on a dusty Spanish playground. But what about communities of adults?

I still think about this occasion when I consider the use of the word 'children' in the New Testament and how it becomes adopted metaphorically to refer to the new Christian community in the Pauline letters. The children are new believers, whose task is to enter the kingdom of God as little children. So the new Christian community can be likened to a family in which everyone is a sibling, 'brothers and sisters' of one another. Reidar Aasgaard points out that 'By using this metaphor he [Paul] says something about Christian relationships, what they are like and what they should be like: in fact, he here appears to disclose elements of his ecclesiological and ethical thinking'.[11] Aasgaard's contention is that other ways of thinking about the Christian community in Pauline theology, such as being the Body of Christ, may have overlooked the importance of the sibling metaphor. This is certainly worth investigation, particularly if we extend the matter of what Christian relationships should be like to the question of the kingdom of God, of eschatological relationships and our ultimate destiny.

In one way this is a very radical concept, because it suggests that the adult religious world, driven by regulation, factionism and forms

---

[10] R. Nye, *Children's Spirituality: What it is and Why it Matters* (London: Church House Publishing, 2009), p. 41.

[11] Aasgaard, *My Beloved Brothers and Sisters*, p. 3.

of exclusion, can be replaced by a sibling-family of a loving parent God in which values such as sharing, love and spiritual growth can be inculcated for a purpose – to manifest the kingdom of God as a fellowship of the children of God, living as children of light (Ephesians 5.8). In such a playground, there is always room for more children, no matter who they are or where they come from. Grace offers you joyful access to the playground, you do not have to earn the right to be there or pay for a ticket. So when we look at theological and ecclesial matters such as those explored in Acts 15, when the new Christians wonder about whether the new religious movement should have the same rules and exclusions as Judaism, we can imagine a new way of thinking entering these very serious issues. In the place where the children of God are together, it doesn't matter what language is spoken by new friends, or where they come from or what happens at their house. What matters is what binds together and what makes it easy to leave what is unnecessary behind.

That is made much easier to see when we consider a group of children being together. On the other hand, the transition from adult roles and relationships to child relationships within the family is difficult and we can see the writers of the Epistles trying to get the communities to see where that transition has not been made effectively. But if the new churches are to be truly Christian, then those child-like relationships have to grow and the adult 'worldly' traits need to disappear. That is not an easy process, because matters of rank, social customs and entrenched ways of thinking are not going to disappear overnight. But the genius of Paul is in pressing new Christians to think differently using metaphors to reframe ways of imagining faith; when Paul talks about the problems of these sibling communities it is in terms of sibling rivalry, squabbling over silly things, which can be solved by the underlying ties of mutuality and love and the generosity of the young towards others: 'we were gentle among you, like a nurse tenderly caring for her own children' (1 Thessalonians 2.7).

> Now before faith came, we were imprisoned and guarded under the law until faith would be revealed. Therefore the law was our disciplinarian until Christ came, so that we might be justified by faith. But now that faith has come, we are no longer subject to a disciplinarian, for in Christ Jesus you are all children of God through faith. As many of you as were baptized into Christ have clothed yourselves with

Christ. There is no longer Jew or Greek, there is no longer slave or free, there is no longer male or female; for all of you are one in Christ Jesus. And if you belong to Christ, then you are Abraham's offspring, heirs according to the promise. (Galatians 3.23–29)

This passage sets the famous words about equality of Christians in context. The 'parent' religion gathers people together by law, but those baptized in Christ are now bound together as a family in which important categories of the adult world no longer apply. Like my children and their Spanish friends, their origins and languages, status, cultural baggage and customs all dissolve in the common commitment to be together, and because the Spirit urges us to play together. There is something of Pentecost in a group of children playing or falling about laughing. Those looking at the disciples thought they were drunk; here were adults expressing themselves like children, filled with joy and mutual experience. It is not surprising then that in Acts 2.14–21 Peter refers to the prophecy of Joel, 'sons and daughters shall prophesy and young men see visions'. The Spirit-filled community recalls to us the enthusiasm and boundless possibility that is continually offered to us by the young: 'Little children, let us love, not in word or speech, but in truth and action' (1 John 3.18). If the world ends suddenly and Jesus returns, then his family will be instantly recognizable and distinctive. The Church should be a graced community, one in which the children know themselves blessed and held by Jesus. I read 1 Corinthians 13.11 as a matter of regret, that Paul senses that the ending of 'being' like a child in adulthood has caused the spiritual sense to dim.[12] We will regain it fully when we stand before God like a child and see him face to face.

That brings us to a very important insight into how the Spirit-filled young family of God as brothers and sisters together look forward to what is to come in meeting God face to face. The letter to the Hebrews says that we are 'brothers and sisters, holy partners in a heavenly calling' (3.1) and that Jesus allies himself with us as his

---

[12] Although in 1 Corinthians 14.20 the injunction is not to be 'children in your thinking; rather, be infants in evil, but in thinking be adults'. Aasgaard, *My Beloved Brothers and Sisters*, p. 280, argues that the play on words in the Greek presses Christians here to be more like adult than child siblings in order to extend the family metaphor to specific parts of the spiritual domain. In the matter of expressed spirituality (prophesying, speaking in tongues) it is important to be more grown up about what this gift conveys to others. Or, we could say, not just babbling.

children: '"Here am I and the children whom God has given me"' (2.13). Where did the writer of Hebrews get that insight? It seems to me that there is another aspect to Jesus' words and actions in insisting the children be brought to him which is of particular importance to the family of God. If God calls us into being and becoming fully human, to have life and life in abundance (John 10.10), and if God never stops calling us to respond 'yes!' in this way, then God also calls us home. But how will we get there? The early Christians expected Jesus to come to fetch them and believed they should be spiritually ready for him, but what does that expectation mean for us today, if the end of time has not yet come?

Dying is a mysterious process and like our birth, unique to each one of us. It may not begin obviously, but it is woven into the ageing process, as our bodies fail. There is a physical sense in which elderly people say that they are ending up like children and none of us wishes for it – loss of bodily control, loss of memory, and dependence on others to function and to get around. However, there is a spiritual side to the end stages of life in which Jesus' words about children cut through our fears and desires. The transition into death needs both surrender and trust, a letting go. But how does that work, and what then?

When, as recounted in Matthew 18, Jesus demands that the disciples stand aside and calls the child to him, presenting the child before them, I think this is more than a demonstration of how attitudes should change in *this* life. I see in this action an eschatological moment. When we die, there can sometimes be an awful lot of 'adults' in the way, family and friends who want us to hang on, doctors and nurses who are trying to keep us alive, even disciples, as in this passage from Matthew 18.2, who are concerned that we understand just how great and important the Lord is and how we must respect him by not bothering him. There may also be our own need for autonomy and control, pushing us firmly back towards the life that is leaving us. In the modern world those adults are very powerful but with the best will in the world they may not understand our real needs. What was it like for that child in the Gospel narrative to stand before those adults? Maybe she could only get glimpses of Jesus between their legs. Perhaps she was confused and flustered by all the voices and instructions to keep away. Perhaps she was trying to work out whom she should obey. Was the Teacher really there, was that him, calling?

132

In the end the adults *have* to get out of the way because Jesus demands it and that is when the child can see and hear clearly. Jesus is there and all his attention is on the child coming to him. There are all sorts of clichés we use for comfort about what happens to people after death: 'safe in the arms of Jesus'; 'in God's bosom'; 'resting in the Lord'; yet these phrases do point us to the sense of the person becoming childlike in the loving presence of God. But I can see an eschatological reality in the human picture of the child taking those steps towards Jesus and being received by him, just as she is, and we can understand how that works by imagining what it was like to be that child and responding to that call to be in Jesus' presence. We have to become like that child – our wealth and knowledge and status will only be hindrances. We take nothing into the world and take nothing out (1 Timothy 6.7). There is a real sense then that children teach us adults how to die – they show us all the things we forget as adults about trust in the presence of the loving parent, who comes when we cry out for him; who waits for us and into whose arms we run with joy. We should learn continually from the children we have around us what we have forgotten because we have put away childish things. It is not surprising then that people sometimes report seeing visions of loved ones before they die. What these people are or are not seeing does not really matter; what they tell us is something about the spiritual state of the dying person, who is becoming like a child. And we know that God does not want any child to die. At the end of our lives it is as children that God dries all our tears, blesses, heals and saves us and calls us into life.

Some questions for reflection

- What 'families' do you feel you belong to? What identifies them as family?
- If you 'count your blessings' what are they?
- What more could we do to help rejected children in today's society?
- What could we do in church/school/the home to bless and privilege children?

Activity

Choose *one* thing arising from your ideas about the final question above and make it happen.

6

Final reflections

The words of God in the world

One of Samuel Beckett's plays is called *Krapp's Last Tape*. In it, an old man replays tapes of his younger self speaking at different points in his life. He realizes that he has forgotten what events meant to him when he was younger and has to look up in a dictionary the word 'viduity' which he cannot now place. But Krapp is making his last tape. Will he make any more or will the words of his life disappear with the hiss at the end of the tape? Will the rest be silence? Krapp reminds us of how much we forget as we age, how we re-write our past and our experiences, and that we can lose important insights, meanings and experiences in the business of making it through to the end of our lives. In Philip Pullman's *His Dark Materials* trilogy, adults can be eaten up by Spectres which consume them as they fall away from the vital, unfixed world of the child.

I think then that our explorations in this book lead us to an idea of children as the words of God in the world: 'children are in a real sense God's language in and through which he reveals his true nature and therefore the nature of his kingdom'.[1] Although children may not be possessed of our sophisticated languages or even able to speak at all, I think that they can be bearers of God's speech about the relation of God in creation to human beings. The five words that I have suggested at the head of each chapter, 'be', 'grow', 'act', 'whole' and 'grace', can be words mediated to us by and through the lives of children.

These are also words that we can twist and damage and destroy. The presence of sin in the world means that we can substitute words like 'die', 'suffer', 'silence', 'break' and 'destroy'. Just a few days'

---

[1] K. White, '"He Placed a Little Child in the Midst"', in M. Bunge (ed.), *The Child in the Bible* (Grand Rapids, MI: Eerdmans, 2008), p. 373.

news will suffice. In August 2012, at the time of writing, I have read about a father killing his children in revenge for his marital troubles with his wife; a child found abandoned in a filthy, cold house, with bleeding nappy rash; a million 'forgotten' children faced with famine in Africa; Romanian orphans who have no hope of ever being adopted; a carer charged with threatening and abusing the children in his care. If children are God's words to us, then we are very good at obliterating that divine speech, twisting it and silencing it.

God's word is good. It has the capacity to take us beyond the mundane to know the playful language of creation, the love and grace of a world that is as God desires it. The laughter of the child playing in the street is God's word.

When we considered how God relates to children, we saw how those children embody hard truths about the way the world is and signs of hope about how it could and should be. Children are everywhere in Scripture, but their lives are often blighted by disease and cut short by death; they are rejected, exploited, ignored, badly treated. Yet where they come into contact with, and are revealed by, the loving purposes of God, they can be the bearers of news about redemption, the initiators of salvation, signs of the essential rightness and goodness at the heart of creation. The despair of Rachel, screaming for her dead children, is counterpointed (but not erased) by the overflowing praise of Hannah, delighting in the living gift of her child. This suggests that Scripture offers vital signposts to how our understanding of and attitudes to children lie at the heart of the way we want the world to be. That in turn reminds us that whatever we discover from Scripture needs to be balanced against the experience of our world *now*. Have we made any progress in making the world as God desires it?

We have explored how God finds children worthy of calling, commission, salvation, healing and blessing. We have struggled with the narratives of biblical texts to find how, in the context of so much child suffering and death, God's life-giving and life-affirming purposes emerge. We can summarize our findings like this:

- God calls all children into life.
- God does not want any child to die.

- God invites all children to be part of the divine will for creation and delights in them.
- God wants children to be whole and happy.
- God's blessing on children privileges them before adults.

It is our job to find ways of responding to these purposes of God in appropriate ways and that means taking children seriously as mediators to us of God's own language. It means taking their spirituality as serious and meaningful and it means working to make sure that children are protected from harm and exploitation as well as making sure they are not smothered by our protection.

Yet all children will become adults. Scripture and theology have given us the understanding that we are all children of God and that no matter how old we are, we are part of God's young family, brothers and sisters in relation to one another in the household of the Mother and Father who is God. As such, the kingdom is offered to us as to children, and it is as spiritual children, learning from real children, that we find ways to understand what kingdom living is all about.

Appendix 1

Words associated with the idea of 'child' in the Bible

Hebrew Scriptures

yoneq   a nursing or suckling child. Used negatively for children under or included in God's judgement, but positively in Psalm 8.2 and Isaiah 11.8

taph   refers to children ranging in age from infants to preadolescents. The word typically means a family member. When the word is applied to non-Israelites it can suggest children from other groups who are under a divine judgement

olel   refers to infants to preadolescents. It can be applied positively to children blessed by God or negatively to children suffering. Can be paired with the word *yoneq* to mean a suckling child

qatan   small or little. Used to mean young, especially to distinguish the younger or youngest

sa'ir   used to mean young, especially to distinguish the younger or youngest

yeled   children. Can be children in general or used for a specific instance. Can also be used in a metaphoric construction, e.g. Hosea 1.2 'children of adultery'

yaldah   children (feminine)

yahid   only child

na'ar   boy, lad or young man, a young servant. Occasionally used metaphorically for a 'child of promise' with a special destiny. Can mean 'the young' or young in years

na'arah   young girl, maid, a young servant

na'ur   the time of a person's youth

bahur   young man or youth

'elem   young man or youth

'ariri   childless

shakkul   childless through the death of existing children; including the metaphor of the she-bear robbed of her cubs

'aqar   unable to have children; barren

rak	'tender' but can be used in the sense of inexperienced, young
'ul	'young' in sense of offspring, like animals have their 'young'. Only with reference to human beings in Isaiah 40.11
ben	son, child, offspring

New Testament

brephos	a baby (including an unborn baby), a newborn or a young child
nepios	a baby or young child. Can also be used metaphorically to denote childlike trust or devotion; new believers learning to grow in faith
nepiazo	to behave like a child
pais	child or servant
paidion	little child. Also appears as a term of affection or as a term for a congregation
paidarion	little child – another diminutive of *pais*
teknon	children. Can be used affectionately towards adults or metaphorically. Can also refer to believers as the children of God
teknion	little child
neos	new (young)
neaniskos	young man
neanias	young man
teknotropheo	to bring up children
teknogoneo	to bear children
ateknos	childless
steira	unable to have children; barren
enkyos	pregnancy: 'expecting'

Appendix 2

List of Scripture passages referring to children

Hebrew Bible

Infants as family members
Gen. 34.29
Num. 31.17, 18
Deut. 2.34; 3.6
1 Sam. 15.3; 22.19
2 Kings 8.12
Job 3.16
Ps. 8.2; 17.14; 137.9
Jer. 6.11; 9.21; 44.7
Lam. 1.5; 2.11, 19, 20;
   4.4
Hos. 13.16
Mic. 2.9
Nah. 3.10

Nursing child
Num. 11.12
Deut. 32.35
1 Sam. 15; 22.19
Ps. 8.2
Song of Sol. 8.1
Isa. 11.8
Jer. 44.7
Lam. 2.11; 4.4
Joel 2.16

Child
1 Sam. 15.3
2 Kings 8.12
Job 3.16

Ps. 137.9
Jer. 6.11; 9.21; 44.7
Lam. 1.5; 2.11, 19, 20
Hos. 13.16
Mic. 2.9
Nah. 3.10

Boy/lad
Gen. 21.12–20; 44.22
Exod. 2.6; 24.5
Num. 11.27
Josh. 8.14
Judg. 13.5
Ruth 2.9
1 Sam. 2.18, 21, 26; 3.1
2 Sam. 14.21
2 Kings 2.23, 24
Job 29.8
Isa. 7.16; 8.4; 40.30
Zech. 2.4

Girl/maid
2 Kings 5.2, 4

The young
Josh. 6.21
2 Chron. 13.7; 34.3
Esth. 3.13
Ps. 37.25
Isa. 20.4
Jer. 51.22
Lam. 2.21

Little one
Gen. 9.22; 42.13
Judg. 9.5
1 Sam. 16.11; 17.14
2 Sam. 9.12

Younger/youngest
Gen. 27.15
2 Chron. 21.17; 22.1
Gen. 29.16; 44.2
1 Sam. 14.49
Judg. 1.13; 3.9; 15.2
Ezek. 16.46; 61
Job 30.1
Gen. 19.31; 25.23; 29.26; 43.33;
    48.14
Josh. 6.26
1 Kings 16.34
Job 32.6

Young/offspring
Isa. 40.11

Youth
Deut. 32.25
Judg. 14.6
Ruth 3.10
1 Sam. 9.2
2 Chron. 36.17
Ps. 78.63
Eccles. 11.9
Isa. 9.17; 40.30
Jer. 6.11
Lam. 1.15
Ezek. 9.6
Joel 2.28
Zech. 9.17

Legislation for youth
Lev. 22.13
Num. 30.3, 16

Early years
1 Sam. 17.33
1 Kings 8.12
Ps. 25.7
Ezek. 4.14
Zech. 13.5

Children
Gen. 21.8
Exod. 1.17; 2.3
1 Kings 17.21
2 Kings 4.18, 26, 34
Ezra 10.1
Neh. 12.43
Job 21.11; 39.3
Eccles. 4.13, 15
Isa. 9.6; 29.3; 51.4
Jer. 31.20
Hos. 1.2

Female children
Gen. 34.4
Joel 3.3
Zech. 8.5

Only child
Gen. 22.2
Judg. 11.34
Jer. 6.26
Zech. 12.10

Childless
Gen. 15.2
Lev. 20.20, 21
Jer. 22.30

Childless through bereavement
2 Sam. 17.18
Prov. 17.12
Isa. 49.20, 21

Jer. 18.29
Hos. 13.8

Barren
Ps. 113.9
Isa. 54.1

Inexperienced
1 Chron. 22.5

Days of youth
Gen. 8.21; 46.34
Prov. 2.17; 5.18
Isa. 54.6
Lam. 3.27
Joel 18
Mal. 2.14

New Testament

Child
Matt. 2.18
Mark 10.24, 29
Luke 1.7; 3.8; 7.35; 20.31
John 8.39
Acts 7.5
1 Cor. 7.14
Eph. 6.1
Col. 3.20
1 Tim. 3.4
Titus 1.6

Children of God (believers)
John 1.12; 11.52
Rom. 8.16; 9.7
1 Cor. 4.14
Gal. 4.25, 27
Eph. 2.3; 5.1
1 Tim. 1.2
1 John 3.10

2 John 1
Rev. 12.4

Little child
Matt. 2.8; 11.16; 14.21; 18.2; 19.13
Mark 5.3; 10.13
Luke 1.59, 66, 76; 2.17; 11.27; 18.16
John 6.9; 13.33; 16.21; 21.5
Gal. 4.19
1 John 2.1, 12, 13, 28; 3.7, 18; 4.4; 5.21
Heb. 2.13; 11.23

Child/servant
Matt. 17.18; 21.15
Luke 2.43; 9.42
Acts 4.27, 30

Baby
Luke 1.41; 2.12; 18.15
Acts 7.19
1 Pet. 2.2
2 Tim. 3.15

Babies
Matt. 11.25; 21.16
Luke 10.21
Rom. 2.20
1 Cor. 3.1
Eph. 4.14
Gal. 4.1
Heb. 5.13

Younger/youngest
Titus 2.6
1 Pet. 5.5
Luke 22.26

Young man
Matt. 19.20
Mark 14.51; 16.5

Luke 7.14
Acts 2.7; 5.6, 10
1 John 2.13
1 Tim. 5.1

Young woman
Titus 2.4
1 Tim. 5.2, 11

Younger son
Luke 15.12
Acts 7.58; 20.9; 23.17

Bring up children
1 Tim. 5.10

Bear children
1 Tim. 5.14

Expecting a child
Luke 2.5

Childless
Luke 20.38

Unable to have children
Luke 1.7, 36; 23.29
Gal. 4.27

Act like a child
1 Cor. 14.20

Bibliography

Aasgaard, R., *My Beloved Brothers and Sisters: Christian Siblingship in Paul* (London: T&T Clark, 2004).

Aasgaard, R., *The Childhood of Jesus: Decoding the Apocryphal Infancy Gospel of Thomas* (Eugene, OR: Cascade Books, 2009).

Allen, L., *Jeremiah: A Commentary* (Louisville, KY: John Knox Press, 2008).

Alter, R., 'Scripture, Commentary and the Challenge of Interpretation', in A. Weiner and L. Kaplan, *Graven Images – on Interpretation: Studies in Culture, Law, and the Sacred* (Madison, WI: University of Wisconsin Press, 2002).

Alter, R., *The Five Books of Moses* (New York: W. W. Norton, 2004).

Alter, R., *The Book of Psalms: A Translation with Commentary* (New York: W. W. Norton, 2007).

Alter, R., *The Wisdom Books: Job, Proverbs and Ecclesiastes* (New York: W. W. Norton, 2010).

Ashe, M., 'Abortion of Narrative: A Reading of the Judgement of Solomon', *Yale Journal of Law and Feminism* 4.81 (1991–1992), pp. 81–92.

Balthasar, H., *Unless You Become Like this Child* (San Francisco: Ignatius Press, 1991).

Barclay, W., *The Gospel of Luke* (Edinburgh: Saint Andrew's Press, 2001 [1953]).

Barton, J. and Muddiman, J., *The Oxford Bible Commentary* (Oxford: Oxford University Press, 2001).

Brueggemann, W., *A Commentary on Jeremiah: Exile and Homecoming* (Grand Rapids, MI: Eerdmans, 1998).

Brueggemann, W., 'Vulnerable Children, Divine Passion and Human Obligation', in M. Bunge, *The Child in the Bible* (Grand Rapids, MI: Eerdmans, 2008).

Bunge, M. (ed.), *The Child in Christian Thought* (Grand Rapids, MI: Eerdmans, 2001).

Bunge, M. (ed.), *The Child in the Bible* (Grand Rapids, MI: Eerdmans, 2008).

Cavaletti, S., *The Religious Potential of the Child* (trans P. and J. Coulter; Mahwah, NJ: Paulist Press, 1983).

Coles, R., *The Spiritual Life of Children* (London: HarperCollins, 1990).

The Complete Jewish Bible with Rashi Commentary online at <www. chabad.org>.

Daily Telegraph: Obituary: Winnie Johnson, available online at <www. telegraph.co.uk/news/obituaries/9486186/Winnie-Johnson.html> (accessed 30 November 2012).

Doctrine Commission of the Church of England, *The Mystery of Salvation* (London: Church House Publishing, 1995).

Donahue, J. and Harrington, D., *Sacra Pagina, The Gospel of Mark* (Collegeville, MN: The Liturgical Press, 2002).

Ehrman, B. and Plese, Z., *The Apocryphal Gospels: Texts and Translation* (Oxford: Oxford University Press, 2011).

Elliott, J. (ed.), *The Apocryphal New Testament: A Collection of Apocryphal Christian Literature in an English Translation based on M. R. James* (Oxford: Oxford University Press, 2005 [1993]).

Ferguson, E., *Baptism in the Early Church: History, Theology, and Liturgy in the First Five Centuries* (Grand Rapids, MI: Eerdmans, 2009).

Ford, D., *The Shape of Living* (London: HarperCollins, 1997).

Fretheim, T., 'God was with the Boy', in M. Bunge, *The Child in the Bible* (Grand Rapids, MI: Eerdmans, 2008).

Fung, R., *The Isaiah Vision: An Ecumenical Strategy for Congregational Evangelism* (Geneva: WCC Publications, 1992).

Gilman, C., 'Female God Language in a Jewish Context', in C. Christ and J. Plaskow (eds), *Womanspirit Rising: A Feminist Reader in Religion* (San Francisco: Harper & Row, 1979).

Gromacki, R., *The Virgin Birth: A Biblical Study of the Deity of Jesus Christ* (Grand Rapids, MI: Kregel Publications, 2002 [1974]).

Gundry-Volf, J., 'The Least and the Greatest: Children in the New Testament', in M. Bunge (ed.), *The Child in Christian Thought* (Grand Rapids, MI: Eerdmans, 2001).

Gwilt, J., 'Biblical Ills and Remedies', *Journal of the Royal Society of Medicine* 79.12 (1986), pp. 738–41.

Hampson, D., *Theology and Feminism* (Oxford: Blackwell, 1990).

Hay, D. and Nye, R., *The Spirit of the Child* (London: HarperCollins, rev. edn 2006; Jessica Kingsley Publications, 1998).

Hernandez, V., 'Argentine Mothers Mark 35 Years Marching for Justice', BBC News 29 April 2012. Available online at <www.bbc.co.uk/news/world-latin-america-17847134> (accessed 30 November 2012).

Herriot, J., *Vets Might Fly* (London: Pan, 2006 [1976]).

Jerome, *Commentary on Jeremiah* (trans. Michael Graves; Ancient Christian Texts; Downers Grove, IL: Inter-Varsity Press, 2012).

Josephus, *Jewish Antiquities* (Ware: Wordsworth Editions, 2006).

Kirby, L., 'Mum's Questions over Tot's Death', *Thurrock Gazette*, 14 October 2011, p. 5 and 'Tot Inquest Ruling', *Thurrock Gazette*, 21 October 2011.

Knowles, D. (ed.), *Augustine: City of God* (Harmondsworth: Penguin, 1980).

Leroi, A., *Mutants: On the Form, Varieties and Errors of the Human Body* (London: HarperCollins, 2003).

Lumen Gentium, online at <www.vatican.va/archive/hist_councils/ii_vatican_council/documents/vat-ii_const_19641121_lumen-gentium_en.html> (accessed 30 November 2012).

McCarthy, B., 'Embryos Cannot be Reduced to Commodities', *The Guardian*, 11 February 2011.

Machen, J., *The Virgin Birth of Christ* (Cambridge: James Clarke & Co., repr. 1987).

McKane, W., *The International Critical Commentary, Jeremiah: Volume 1: 1–25* (Edinburgh: T&T Clark, 1986).

Marsh, B., 'Dozens of Babies being Born to Mothers over Fifty', *Daily Telegraph* 8 May 2006. Available online at <www.telegraph.co.uk/news/uknews/3339190/Dozens-of-babies-being-born-to-mothers-over-50.html#.Tpa9kbmfVLU.email> (accessed 30 November 2012).

Messer, N., *Respecting Life: Theology and Bioethics* (London: SCM, 2011).

Mischel, W., 'Processes in Delay of Gratification', in L. Berkowitz (ed.), *Advances in Experimental Social Psychology* (vol. 7; San Diego, CA: Academic Press, 1974).

Mischel, W., Shoda, Y. and Rodriguez, M., 'Delay of Gratification in Children', *Science* 244 (1989), pp. 933–8.

Moran, C., *How to be a Woman* (London: Ebury Press, 2011).

Moran, C., 'A Woman's Right to Choose', *The Times* Magazine, 17 March 2012.

Nye, R., *Children's Spirituality: What it is and Why it Matters* (London: Church House Publishing, 2009).

O'Rourke, K. and Boyle, P., *Medical Ethics: Sources of Catholic Teachings* (Washington: Georgetown University Press, 4th edn, 2011).

Platt, J., Judgement of Judge John Platt in the Romford County Court 2012. Available online at <www.bailii.org/ew/cases/Misc/2012/15.html> (accessed 30 November 2012).

Privett, P. and Richards, A. (eds), *Through the Eyes of a Child* (London: Church House Publishing, 2009).

Pullman, P., *The Good Man Jesus and the Scoundrel Christ* (London: Viking, 2010).

Radner, E., 'Blessing: A Scriptural and Theological Reflection', a paper presented to the clergy conference of the Diocese of Ontario on 16 June 2009. Available online at <http://fulcrum-anglican.org.uk/page.cfm?ID=436> (accessed 13 August 2012).

Ratcliff, D. (ed.), *Children's Spirituality: Christian Perspectives, Research and Applications* (Eugene, OR: Cascade Books).

Renton, A., 'A Letter to God – and a Reply from Lambeth', *The Times*, 22 April 2011.

Rozenberg, J., 'Suffer the Little Children to Come unto Me', *The Guardian*, 8 August 2012. Available online at <www.guardian.co.uk/law/2012/aug/08/jewish-girl-baptism> (accessed 16 August 2012).

St Ambrose, *De institutione virginis et sanctae Mariae virginitate perpetua ad Eusebium.*

Smart, C., 'Jubilate Agno', in M. Walsh, *Selected Poems of Christopher Smart* (Manchester: Carcanet Press, 1979).

Stanford, P. (ed.), *The Death of a Child* (London: Continuum, 2011).

Stortz, M., '"Where or When was your Servant Innocent?"' in M. Bunge, *The Child in Christian Thought* (Grand Rapids, MI: Eerdmans, 2001).

Trible, P., *Texts of Terror: Literary-Feminist Readings of Biblical Narratives* (Minneapolis: Fortress Press, 1984).

Turner, H., 'Expository Problems: The Virgin Birth', *The Expository Times* 68 (October 1956), pp. 12–17.

Vermes, G., *The Authentic Gospel of Jesus* (London: Folio Society, 2009).

Welburn, A., *From a Virgin Womb: The Apocalypse of Adam and the Virgin Birth* (Leiden: Brill, 2008).

White, K., '"He Placed a Little Child in the Midst"', in M. Bunge (ed.), *The Child in the Bible* (Grand Rapids, MI: Eerdmans, 2008).

Williams, F. (trans.), *The Panarion of Epiphanius of Salamis* (Leiden: Brill, 1993).

Williams, R., *Lost Icons* (Edinburgh: T&T Clark, 2000).

Journals

International Journal of Children's Spirituality (Routledge)
Journal of Childhood and Religion (Sopher Press)

Useful websites

www.nspcc.org.uk
www.childline.org.uk
www.childrenssociety.org.uk
www.barnardos.org.uk
www.godlyplay.org/uk
www.messychurch.org.uk
www.churchofengland.org/our-views/medical-ethics-health-social-care-policy.aspx
www.miscarriageassociation.org.uk
www.infertilitynetworkuk.com
www.malefertility.co.uk